Love's Funny That Way

Also by Judy Brown

1,349 Hilarious Jokes

Funny You Should Say That

Funniest Jokes from the World's Best Comedians

Jokes to Go

She's So Funny

It's a Man's World

LOve's Funny THat WAy

800 TERRIFIC JOKES ABOUT ROMANCE AND RELATIONSHIPS

Judy Brown

Sterling Publishing, New York

Published by Sterling Publishing Co., Inc.
387 Park Avenue South, New York, NY 10016

© 2006 by Judy Brown

Distributed in Canada by Sterling Publishing
c/o Canadian Manda Group, 165 Dufferin Street
Toronto, Ontario, Canada M6K 3H6

Distributed in Great Britain by Chrysalis Books
64 Brewery Road, London N7 9NT, England

Distributed in Australia by Capricorn Link (Australia) Pty. Ltd.
P.O. Box 704, Windsor, NSW 2756, Australia

Sterling ISBN 1-4027-3525-1

Library of Congress Cataloging-in-Publication Data upon request

1 3 5 7 9 8 6 4 2

Manufactured in the United States of America

* FOREWORD *

Dating, love, and marriage are all an inescapable part of the social fabric—if you haven't yet been there, done that, and collected someone's T-shirt to sleep in, your parents have.

It can sort of be summed up as follows: When we meet someone we think we like, we make a reality check by asking ourselves "Do I?" If things proceed nicely from there, we are likely to find ourselves before witnesses, declaring "I do!" At some point thereafter, however, almost all of us wind up asking ourselves: "What did I do?"

What more can anyone say, except "Love's funny that way"—and when it's not, you can pick up this book to laugh out loud, mock Cupid, and remind yourself you're not alone.

Have fun,
Judy Brown

For info on comedy topics of all sorts, including my other joke books, comedy seminars, and publishing workshops:

e-mail: judy@judybrown.info
Web site: www.judybrown.info

* ACKNOWLEDGMENTS *

First, I'd like to thank the comedians who have managed to turn their love lives into laughter.

And *gracias* to my editor, Stuart Miller, who agreed with me that love, dating, and marriage can be a joke.

Love's Funny That Way

* ADULTERY *

In order to stop themselves from cheating, some guys carry around a picture of their wife so they can pull it out and remind themselves of what they have. That didn't work for me, so I carry around a picture of my wife's attorney.

— Jason Love

You can't just have an adultery, you "commit" adultery. And you can't commit adultery unless you already have a commitment. Once you commit, then you can commit the adultery—and then you get caught, get divorced, lose your mind, and they have you committed.

— Jerry Seinfeld

My ex-husband cheated on me, even though I was a good wife and mother; I cleaned, I cooked. The way to a man's heart may be through his stomach, but that's only if you twist the blade and lift up.

— Sheila Kay

As you get older, you get less picky about who you date. I have this Jewish friend who five years ago, swore he was only going to marry a nice Jewish girl. Today he's willing to settle for a slutty Palestinian.

— *Andrea Henry*

As you get older, the pickings get slimmer, but the people don't.

— *Carrie Fisher*

There are things I used to be able to do when I was younger that I can't anymore. Like have a conversation with my wife without getting yelled at.

— *Reno Goodale*

You know you're getting old when the only thing you've got in the house from Victoria's Secret is their catalog.

— *Joan Rivers*

I was talking to this cute young woman who said she had a thing for older men. I got all excited and asked, "What's that?" She said, "Pepper spray."

— *Chuck Johnson*

I didn't realize I was getting old until my attorney advised me to get my affairs in order. OK, so now I have Andy on Monday, Bob on Tuesday, and the FedEx man on Wednesday.

— Katherine Poehlmann

I've always dated older men. But it's gotten to the point that if I want to date someone older than me, I'll have to go to the cemetery and dig him up.

— Tonya Moon

My grandmother's ninety. She's dating. He's ninety-three. They're very happy, they never argue. They can't hear each other.

— Cathy Ladman

I've got an older uncle who's ninety-two, and I've learned something about that age: their whole social life is going to funerals. Somebody dies, they call a date. "Hey, Margaret, Bob died. We're all going, the whole gang." And why not? The funeral home is a great place to go when you're ninety-two : free parking, well-lit, somebody opens the door, free coffee downstairs, and there's always somebody a little worse off than you.

— John David Sidley

It isn't so enjoyable going horseback riding, is it? The smell is horrible, he always has his nose in another horse's ass, and he's completely indifferent to the fact that I'm sitting on him. I might as well be married.

— Sue Schwartz

The Discovery Channel had a fascinating show on the mating habits of hyenas. They said that the male hyena often will get angry at the female hyena while they are having sex. It doesn't help that the female hyena is laughing at you all the time.

— Jay Leno

I read that when rabbits are having sex, the male rabbit screams, rolls over on his side, and faints. That's reassuring. Because now when I'm driving my car and see a rabbit on the side of the road, I know he's not dead, he just had a date.

— Cathy Ladman

* ANNIVERSARIES *

Here's some advice for you married guys. If you're looking for an anniversary gift for your wife, a didgeridoo is not a good choice, even if it's handmade.

— *Reno Goodale*

I was married for four years. I was hoping the marriage would last for five, because the gift for five is wood. "Honey, you're so special, I got you twenty feet of 1" by 8".

— *Carol Leifer*

The symbol for the seventh anniversary is rust.

— *Ellen Orchid*

We've just marked our tenth wedding anniversary on the calendar, and threw darts at it.

— *Phyllis Diller*

My husband and I celebrated our thirty-eighth wedding anniversary. You know what I finally realized? If I had killed the man the first time I thought about it, I'd have been out of jail by now.

— *Anita Milner*

It's really hard with lesbian relationships to know when your anniversary date is. Is it your first date? The first time you go to bed together? Is it the day you move in? Lucky for my girlfriend and me, all those things happened at the same time.

— Lynda Montgomery

* ARGUMENTS *

I got into an argument with my girlfriend inside a tent. A tent is not a good place for an argument. I tried to walk out on her and had to slam the flap.

— Mitch Hedberg

Never go to bed mad. Stay up and fight.

— Phyllis Diller

I don't know where my wife went to learn how to argue, but she really got good at it there.

— John Heffron

My ex-wife and I argued so much that we started repeating ourselves. We should have just taped the shouting and let the recorders fight it out amongst themselves. Then I could have told some guy at a bar, "I'm not really here. I'm at home arguing with my wife."

— Jason Love

Fighting in marriage is so hard. I get mad at my husband, and where am I gonna go? "I'm leaving 'sniff'...to the kitchen. And I'm staying there until you apologize!" Because it could be a long time, and at least I've chosen the room that has food.

— Laurie McDermott

My wife and I have a system for settling arguments: we just talk and talk until she's right.

— Jason Love

After a fight I'd bring my wife one red rose. Of all the presents you can get a woman there really is nothing like that one rose to say, "Honey, sweetheart, this is just to let you know I'm so cheap."

— Daniel Liebert

My parents only had one argument in forty-five years. It lasted forty-three years.

— Cathy Ladman

Sex after a fight is often the best there is, which is why you're never allowed in the locker room right after a prizefight.

— Jay Leno

We got in such a bad argument one day, I slept at the house of a mutual friend, Blake. Now my wife won't talk to Blake because he was harboring a fugitive.

— Jason Love

* ASTROLOGY *

I went to an astrologer to see if she could tell me who I would be most compatible with, and she said I attract Virgos, Leos, and psychos.

— Zorba Jevon

* BACHELOR PARTIES *

My fiancé wanted a bachelor party, but I said no way. Guys always claim, "that's my last night of freedom." I don't think so. Your last night of freedom was the one *before* you proposed.

— Denise Munro Robb

* BACHELORETTE PARTIES *

I was at this club, full of a rowdy bachelorette party.
The bride was so drunk her veil was hanging in her
margarita. It was disgusting, I finally said, "Ma'am, as
many times as I've been married, I've never gone out
and gotten drunk the night before the wedding. I
always thought about the baby."

— Vicki Barbolak

* BARS *

I went to a bar and this guy comes up to me and
says, "You're moderately attractive." So I told him he
resembled an asshole.

— Jeremy Michaels

Instead of buying me a drink, this guy offered me a sip of his. Talk about a fear of commitment.

— Caroline Rhea

Generally not a good idea, meeting guys in a bar. It's like going grocery shopping when you're hungry; you bring home stuff you don't need.

— Cory Kahaney

I went up to a girl in a bar once and asked her where she was from. I guess she wasn't interested, because she said, "Mars." So I asked, "You need a ride home?"

— Ray Romano

Guys should know that they're having a bad night in the bar when we break out the fake names. I'm not even discreet about it, "I'm Marsha, this is Jan, and that's Cindy. Our friend Alice is in the bathroom."

— Christina Walkinshaw

* BIOLOGICAL CLOCKS *

My girlfriend is at that stage where her biological clock is telling her it's time for her to be making me feel guilty and immature.

— Kevin Hench

In the spring, I was waiting for a friend and happened to witness a male hummingbird chase after a female hummingbird for about ten minutes. Finally, the female hummingbird got tired, gave up and just let the male hummingbird do whatever he wanted. And I thought, "Ah, college."

— *Wendy Wilkins*

Marriage is hard. Monogamy is really difficult. When you look around the animal kingdom very few creatures mate for life. Maybe swans, and everyone knows swans are angry. They've been married so long, they'll bite you.

— *Fiona Walsh*

Eagles mate while flying at eighty miles an hour. And when they start to drop, they don't stop until the act is completed. So, it's not uncommon they both hit the ground and die. That's how committed they are. Boy, don't we feel like wimps for stopping to answer the phone? I don't know about you, but if I'm one of those two birds and we're getting close to the ground, I would seriously consider faking it.

— Ellen DeGeneres

I don't even consider myself bisexual. I just think of myself as a "people person."

— Michael Dane

Am I gay? Am I straight? And I realized: I'm just slutty! Where's my parade?

— Margaret Cho

Why do we fix people up? You thought they'd have a good time, and it's a little power trip for you. You're playing God. And of course, God was the first to fix people up, God fixed up Adam and Eve. "She's nice. She's very free about her body, doesn't wear much. She was going out with a snake, but I think that's over."

— Jerry Seinfeld

I get no respect. I had a blind date. I waited two hours on the corner. A girl walked by. I said "Are you Louise?" She said, "Are you Rodney?" I said, "Yeah." She said, "I'm not Louise."

— **Rodney Dangerfield**

I've been on so many blind dates I should get a free dog.

— **Wendy Liebman**

* BOOKS *

Trying to date in this day and age without a handbook is a lot like a sperm trying to navigate its way through a vasectomy.

— **Debbie Kasper**

I buy relationship books. You've heard of *Women Who Love Too Much?* I thought it was *Women Who Love to Munch.* I got the wrong book and put on a few pounds, which didn't help.

— **Robin Roberts**

I'm dating again, but it's got me confused. So I've been reading up on the differences between men and women. I read *The Rules,* the Mars and Venus books, *Dating for Dummies.* And here's the real difference: women buy the books.

— Daryl Hogue

I bought a book *Dating for Dummies* because thought I'd see a picture of my ex in it. Nope, just a photo of me.

— Jayne Warren

Have you heard of this new book titled *1,001 Sex Secrets Men Should Know?* It contains comments from 1,001 different women on how men can be better in bed. I think that women would actually settle for three: Slow down, turn off the TV, call out the right name.

— Jay Leno

If I ever wrote a sex manual, it would be called, "Ouch, You're on My Hair."

— Richard Lewis

* BOYFRIENDS *

I don't even want a boyfriend. I just want someone to see my underwear because it's so pretty.

— Carmen Lynch

Everyone thinks they know what they want from a relationship. I've got my shopping list for the boyfriend store: he's gotta be cute, smart, smell good, and not in that aftershave way, but with those guy pheromones that make you want to tuck your head under his shoulder, sniff, and go, "*Aaahh!*" He shouldn't live too far away, he should think I'm funny, have a job of some sort, and oh, the most important thing...he can't be imaginary.

— **Janet Rosen**

I'm in my thirties and I've never really had a boy-friend. I always chose the wrong men, so now I have an imaginary boyfriend. The problem is I can't count on him. If I need someone to lean on and choose him, I fall over.

— **Penelope Lombard**

Boyfriend. This is such a weird word. There's no good word about someone if you're not married. Even calling a guy you live with your boyfriend makes you sound eleven years old. Old man? If you're not living with Willie Nelson, that one doesn't work, either.

— **Elayne Boosler**

My boyfriend is pressuring me to get pregnant, but I'm not sure it's such a good idea. Because he's already got a wife and three kids. Plus my husband's not too crazy about the idea either.

— Andrea Henry

I come from Florida where there are only two dating options: criminals and guys over ninety. My first boyfriend was an accessory to a 7-Eleven hold-up. He drove the getaway car. Such a nothing crime. You could practically put that on your business cards, "Getaway Limousine Service: When You Need to Get the Hell Outta There FAST!"

— Andi Rhoads

My last boyfriend — it was one of those things that you know isn't going to work, but you think you maybe should hold on until your birthday.

— Karith Foster

We were incompatible in a lot of ways. Like for example, I was a night person, and he didn't like me.

— Wendy Liebman

I've never kept a boyfriend longer than a car.

— Janice J. Heiss

* BRAS *

My favorite marketing gimmick, the WonderBra. Doesn't your date notice that your chest feels like a stuffed animal? And what happens when you get home and take it off? It's called the WonderBra because the guy is sitting there thinking, "I wonder where her boobs went?"

— Rebecca Nell

I stuff my bra. So if you get to second base with me, you'll find that the bases are loaded.

— Wendy Liebman

* BREAKING UP *

Breaking up is like knocking over a coke machine. You can't do it in one push. You've gotta rock it back and forth a few times, and then it goes over.

— Jerry Seinfeld

I have two brothers and boys can do no wrong in my mother's eyes. When they broke up with someone it was always, "You can do better. She wasn't good enough for you." But when I broke up with a guy she'd be like, "You shouldn't be so picky. So it was a stolen car, at least he picked you up."

— Lori Giarnella

Timing is everything in relationships. Halloween is the pre-holiday season cutoff for breaking up. The best time to date is from Easter through Labor Day, because there are no major holidays which involve gift giving. So you can start your breakup by Labor Day, and still have six weeks for the whole back-and-forth breakup/get-back-together/breakup routine before Halloween.

— Caryl Fuller

I hate the way relationships end. There's always that double-meaning lawyer speech: "We have to talk." Strangely enough, that's the exact same thing President Truman said to the Japanese before he dropped the bomb. Then you have the other classic breakup line. "Let's still be friends." Which means, "If you still want to buy me stuff, I'm OK with that."

— Devin Dugan

How about this breakup line? "I love you, but we can't be together." I say, "So I guess when you hate me, you'll call me, and we can be a couple again."

— Michele Balan

I was going with someone for a few years but we broke up. It was one of those things. He wanted to get married, and I didn't want him to.

— Rita Rudner

My last relationship, I was always there for her and she dumped me. I said, "Remember when your grandma died? I was there. Remember when you flunked out of school? I was there. Remember when you lost your job? I was there!" She said, "I know, you're bad luck."

— Tom Arnold

There is one thing I would break up over, and that is if she caught me with another woman. I wouldn't stand for that.

— Steve Martin

I broke up with my boyfriend of five years. We would have broken up after the first two weeks, but new restaurants kept opening.

— Jann Karam

If you're going to break up with your old lady, and you live in a small town, make sure you don't break up at three in the morning. Because you're screwed, there's nothing to do. So make it about nine in the morning. Bullshit around, worry her a little, then come back at seven in the night.

— Lenny Bruce

I had to break up with someone I was casually dating. But I couldn't say, "I think we should see other people," because we were already doing that. So I said, "You know that seeing other people thing we do? I really like that. We should do more of that, exclusively. It's not you, it's me. Because I don't like you."

— Steve Hofstetter

My family made me break it off with my boyfriend, it was just too much for them. They couldn't handle me being Greek, and him being imaginary.

— Andrea Henry

I just broke up with my girlfriend, because I caught her lying. Under another man.

— Doug Benson

If you want to get rid of a man, I suggest saying, "I love you. I want to marry you. I want to have your children." Sometimes they leave skid marks.

— Rita Rudner

Jesus must have had a hard time with women. Because there would be no good way to break up with Jesus. "No, it's not you, it's me. Of course I love you, but only as a savior. You can never be anything more to me than that!"

— Geoff Holtzman

Refusal to accept reality does not change reality. My girlfriend broke up with me. I said, "I can't imagine you leaving me." She said, "Well, let me help. You stay here. I'm going to turn around. Then I'm going to start walking. To you, it'll seem like I'm getting smaller."

— **Basil White**

You never know when things are going to get bad in your relationship. You find out that your lover is planning an intimate weekend for two in the woods... so there will be no witnesses. "Honey, why did you pack the gun? It's not hunting season."

— **Mike Cotayo**

My girlfriend and I recently broke up. Apparently she didn't like it when I introduced her as an "acquaintance" of mine. That, and the lying and cheating.

— **Douglas Gale**

I broke up with my girlfriend. She moved in with another guy, and I draw the line at that.

— **Garry Shandling**

My boyfriend and I broke up because I went over to his house unannounced. He was upset that I'd come over without calling first, especially since he was there with another woman. He trusted me, and I let him down.

— **Grace White**

I wasn't the easiest guy to live with, I had multiple personalities, but what bothered her was that none of them made any money.

— Daniel Liebert

I just dumped my boyfriend. I found some chick's stilettos under his bed. I won't date a man who has a timeshare in his pants.

— Elaine Pelino

I once had a man break up with me. He said I was using him because right after making love I would weigh myself.

— Emily Levine

A woman broke up with me, and sent me pictures of her and her new boyfriend in bed together.
Solution? I sent them to her dad.

— Christopher Case

When men break up they want to remain friends. Why? Why can't they just get lost?

— Rita Rudner

I burned a lot of CDs for my girlfriend. When she broke up with me, I burned them all.

— Troy Conrad

After you've dated someone it should be legal to stamp them with what's wrong with them, so the next person doesn't have to start from scratch.

— Rita Rudner

After a breakup, I'll date anyone. If a one-legged troll who lives under a bridge glances at me twice: it's Mardi Gras!

— Kris McGaha

How many people still have that relationship with their ex, where you call each other up just to yell? It's like you're married: you're not having sex, and you're fighting.

— Rosie Tran

The last girl I went out with blew me off. Now I call her with lame excuses to see her, "Hey, did I leave a penny over there?"

— David Spade

I stay friends with my ex-boyfriends. It's like i'm the queen of recycling, but I don't know how to get rid of hazardous waste.

— Eileen Budd

I broke up with someone, and she said, "You'll never find anyone like me again." And I'm thinking, I hope not! If I don't want you, why would I want someone just like you? Does anybody end a bad relationship and say, "By the way, do you have a twin?"

— Larry Miller

I asked my ex-girlfriend, "Do you think we'll get back together?" She said, "I think the chances are better of me putting Super Unleaded into a rented car."

— David Spade

If you had a relationship with someone and you try to become friends afterwards, it's difficult. Because you know each other's tricks. It's like magicians, trying to entertain one another. "Look, a rabbit." "So? I believe this is your card." "Why don't we just saw each other in half, and call it a night?"

— Jerry Seinfeld

When you get back together with an old boyfriend, it's pathetic. It's like having a garage sale and buying your own stuff back.

— Laura Kightlinger

I had the best day ever: I ran into my ex-boyfriend and his new girlfriend. With my car.

— **Karen Anderson**

I spotted my ex-boyfriend at the mall. We had a really bad breakup, and I didn't want to make eye contact with him. Thank God I've had years of waitress training.

— **Kate Mason**

My ex-boyfriend's mother told me that I hate men. I said, "I don't hate all men, just your son. That's just one guy."

— **Laura Kightlinger**

* BREASTS *

I read in *Cosmopolitan* that women like to have whipped cream sprayed on their breasts during sex. Unfortunately, my girlfriend has silicone implants. So I use non-dairy topping.

— **Jeff Shaw**

A lot of guys think the larger a woman's breasts are, the less intelligent she is. I think it's the opposite. I think the larger a woman's breasts are, the less intelligent the men become.

— **Anita Wise**

Scientists now believe that the primary biological function of breasts is to make males stupid.

— Dave Barry

* BRIDAL SHOWERS *

When my sister got married I threw her a bridal shower. What a nifty way to spend a Sunday afternoon, right, ladies? My aunt bought my sister a spice rack, and thought it would be nice idea to individually wrap all the spices. So for forty-five minutes we were going, *"Ooooh, paprika!"*

— Rosie O'Donnell

What's a bridal shower if you're gay? It's the parade of gifts you'll never get because you're homosexual. "Come in and take a look at the blender, toaster, silverware you'll have to buy yourself." I hate that. I don't bring a gift anymore, I take one. I have six Cuisinarts. I don't give a shit, they owe us.

— Suzanne Westenhoever

* BRIDESMAIDS *

I hate the saying "Always a bridesmaid, never a bride." I like to put it into perspective by thinking, "Always a pallbearer, never a corpse."

— Laura Kightlinger

I was a recently a bridesmaid in my best friend's wedding. Here's what I learned: brides are crazy! But I didn't mind spending $250 on a dress because she had an open bar, so that pretty much evened out.

— *Tamara Pennington*

I hate being a bridesmaid, because I have to dress to the bride's taste. My best friend sent me this black-purple, floor-length dress, two sizes small. I shuffled down the aisle like the Bridesmaid of Frankenstein. Just wait until I get married. Lucky Charms are my favorite cereal, and you're going as a Leprechaun bridesmaid, bitch.

— *Tamara Castle*

* BROTHERS *

I should understand men better than I do, because I grew up with brothers. I wanted sisters; they're better for a girl. They teach you how to put on makeup, how to do your hair, give you dating tips. You know what brothers teach you? How to unhook a bra with your teeth.

— *Carol Siskind*

I can never sound cool talking to women. I can't say, "The Benz is broken, we'll have to take the Beemer." With me, it's more like, "My skateboard is trashed, we'll be taking the Nikes."

— Geoff Holtzman

A guy knows he's in love when he loses interest in his car for a couple of days.

— Tim Allen

I've never known a man who wasn't deeply attached on a very emotional level to his beloved vehicle. Whether it was a piece of junk or a masterpiece made no difference. They rode in their metal boxes and were in control of their lives. I think I know why so many men are afraid to make a commitment to women. It's because we can't be steered.

— Rita Rudner

Men look at women the way men look at cars. Every-one looks at Ferraris. Now and then we like a pickup truck. And we all end up with a station wagon.

— Tim Allen

I have a boyfriend and four male cats, so basically I have five male cats. They all demand to be fed the moment I set foot in the house, followed by heavy petting.

— Andi Rhoads

The cheap dates always cloak themselves as roman-tics. This one dude used to give me one rose, and he had a corny line to go along with it. "I give you one rose because you are one special lady." After a cou-ple dates I was like, "No, you give me one rose because you're one cheap bastard."

— Wanda Sykes

Boy was my ex-wife cheap! For my birthday she was going to get me a Greek fisherman's hat, but he woke up.

— Daniel Liebert

Men are so cheap these days. Whatever happened to guys bringing women chocolates or flowers? I've reached the point where the Grim Reaper could show up at my door and I'd be like, "Oh my God, you brought me a scythe. That's so sweet!"

— Jenée

My all-time favorite cheap date happened during the time I lived in New Jersey. He used to back up to the toll so that the booth would be on my side.

— Wanda Sykes

My father was so cheap. When my parents were engaged, he didn't give my mother a diamond ring. He gave her a lump of coal and told her to be patient.

— Cathy Ladman

My husband Fang was the cheapest man alive. My wedding ring turned my whole body green. My engagement ring, he said it was a square-cut emerald: it was a Chiclet.

— Phyllis Diller

* CHEATING *

Dating two men at the same time is fun if you like doing twice as much work. I think people who cheat are stupid. One boyfriend is too much for me, two is a part-time job.

— Rosie Tran

My girlfriend found out I was messing around with this other chick. So she called my wife.

— Corey Holcomb

* CHOCOLATE *

Chocolate releases endorphins; when you eat chocolate it feels like being in love. I was lonely, so I bought a Hershey's Bar. I opened it up, but printed on the wrapper it said, "I just want to be friends."

— Denise Munro Robb

* CLICHES *

I always wanted to be the last guy on earth, just to see if all those women were lying to me.

— Ronnie Shakes

Benjamin Franklin was wrong. In my experience, "Early to bed, and early to rise," makes a man dull, anal and horny.

— Gloria Brinkworth

When somebody says to you, "The last thing I want to do is hurt you," what they really mean is, "It's on the list. I've just got some other things to do first."

— Mark Schiff

They say that it's the thought that counts. Yeah, right. Try showing up at your girlfriend's place with a dozen thoughts. "Oh, you shouldn't have." "I didn't."

— Adam Richmond

* CLOTHING *

What if one day the stars aligned and I managed to put on a matching outfit? Wouldn't my wife wonder, "Who picked that out? You couldn't have. Are you seeing someone else?"

— Jeff Scott

* COLOGNE *

What are men wearing? Why do they think women like horse saddles and pine sap? If a man wanted me to follow him down the street, he should wear something called "Butter Cookie" or even better, "Croissant."

— Rita Rudner

* COMMANDMENTS *

I'm glad God gave the Ten Commandments to a man. A woman would have thought, "I know that's what he said, but I don't think that's what he meant."

— Diane Nichols

* COMMITMENT *

Committing is hard for men. I can't even commit to one TV program. I get this nervous feeling that there's something better on another channel.

— Jason Love

I was sleeping with this guy who had such a fear of committing to me that he married his fiancée.

— Debbie Kasper

I was so impressed with the level of commitment he showed that I went out for coffee with my stalker. "You followed me for eighty blocks on the bus? No-body I've ever dated would do that." But ladies, you want to get rid of a stalker? Go out with him. Then he becomes like a regular guy and never calls back.

— *Ann Design*

* COMMUNICATION *

Men say women talk too much. Women don't talk too much, men just listen too little.

— *Rosie Tran*

When a man says, "We've got to talk," the woman hears, "We're going to have a nice conversation." When a woman says, "We've got to talk," a man hears, "Will the defendant please rise?"

— *Peter Sasso*

A lot of women say we men don't pay enough attention to real ancient ships. At least I think this is what they're saying. Maybe these women should speak more clearly.

— *The Covert Comic*

* CONFIDENCE *

You get more confident when you're married. When you're single and you don't hear from your boyfriend, you wonder, "Should I call him?" When you're married and you don't hear from your husband, you wonder *what* you should call him.

— Rita Rudner

* CONTRACEPTION *

For a single woman, the most effective method of oral contraception is to just yell out, "Yes, yes, I want to have your baby!"

— Marsha Doble

My husband and I found this great new method of birth control that really, really works...Every night before we go to bed we spend an hour with our kids.

— Roseanne Barr

Read the condom boxes, they're pretty funny. Trojans say, "New shape." I didn't know this was necessary. Another box said, "Reservoir," I said. "You mean these things can actually generate hydroelectric power?" I saw this new great brand: extra-super-sensitive condoms. I thought, "Wow! These must hang around and talk to you after the guy leaves."

— Elayne Boosler

I opened my stuffed dresser drawer, and a box of condoms fell out of the back, and landed at the bottom of the dresser. And I thought, "This is my sex life: it's gotten so bad, my condoms are committing suicide." And the worst part is, they left a note. "Dear Larry: No one should ever be made to feel this useless for this long. Yours in misery, the Trojan Variety Pack."

— Larry Getlen

I'm Catholic. My mother and I were unpacking and she found my diaphragm. I had to tell her it was a bathing cap for my cat.

— Lizz Winstead

Japanese women are refusing to take birth control pills, opting to leave contraception up to men. Do you know what they call women who leave birth control up to men? Mothers.

— Jennifer Vally

You know what's the worst contraceptive? The Pill. Because you have to keep taking it every day, regardless of what's going on in your love life. It's so nice during those two-year lulls to have a daily reminder. "I sleep alone, but oh my, look, it's time for my loser pill." Can you imagine if men had to wear a condom for thirty days just in case they might need it? "It's day twenty-eight, but somebody might call."

— *Caroline Rhea*

* COOKING *

A word of advice for women. Go with a guy who cooks. Trust me, I've dated extensively and had a few husbands, and I know what I'm talking about. If you teach a man to fish he'll fish all damn day. But marry a man who likes to cook fish, and you've not only got poached salmon crepes for breakfast, but he also does the shopping.

— *Christine Blackburn*

* COSMETICS *

Lipsticks have names; my new one is called "Desire."
I asked my husband what he thought about it, but
he's kind of an old hippie and said, "Your lipstick is
too dark." I replied, "Yeah, and your opinion is too
loud." Now I've got a new lipstick in a much frostier
shade, called "Sleep on the Couch, Mister Natural."

— Janet Rosen

* DATING *

I think women have it much easier than men on the
first date. Because they still have to call us up. That
means they like us, they called. Nobody ever calls
you to say, "I won't be dating you."

— Diane Nichols

I asked this one girl out and she said, "You got a
friend?" I said yes, she said, "Then go out with him."

— Dom Irrera

I was in a club the other night. A woman actually
asked me out. She said, "You: out!"

— Steve Smith

I don't get no respect. A girl phoned me and said, "Come on over, there's nobody home." I went over. Nobody was home.

— **Rodney Dangerfield**

I dated a guy who answered the door naked. He said, "My life's an open book." I said, "I think about all you've got there is a small brochure."

— **Robin Roberts**

There are four basic questions you should ask before a man takes you out. If he answers "yes" to any, reconsider the advantages of being alone: "Do you know the meaning of the word 'postal' and do you consider it a recreational activity? Have you ever been considered a good candidate for a movie made for the Lifetime channel? Do you have a surf-board, skateboard, snowboard or large hat with beer straw in your truck? Do you live in your truck?"

— **Jackie Newton**

My Dad hasn't dated since the 1940s, so some of his advice is old-fashioned. He says things like, "If you really want to get to know the woman you're going out with, take her to the beach: if anything is fake it will float."

— **Blomo Risher**

How many of you ever started dating someone because you were too lazy to commit suicide?

— **Judy Tenuta**

Dating is a lot like sports. You have to practice, you work out, you study the greats. You hope to make the team, and it hurts to be cut.

— Sinbad

Guys, on a first date don't just brag about yourself, take a real interest in her, "So what are your plans for the future? Gonna eat that pickle?"

— Daniel Liebert

What is a date really, but a job interview that lasts all night? The only difference is that in not many job interviews is there a chance you'll wind up naked.

— Jerry Seinfeld

Some women are always thinking about getting married, even on the first date. Not me, I go straight to thinking about the funeral.

— Denise Munro Robb

Dating goes in stages. The first is the best. Conversation is new, conversation exists. You go to a restaurant, the girl goes to sit down, the guy pulls the chair out, puts the chair back in. Six, seven months go by, "What? You think I work here? Sit down and don't order the lobster, okay?"

— John Mendoza

On a first date, usually guys take you to a movie where you sit in the dark staring at a screen, not speaking to each other. Makes perfect sense, it prepares you for marriage.

— Denise Munro Robb

I went out on a first date with a guy who felt the need to tell me he was taking anger management classes. I didn't know whether to be scared, or respect the fact that he was trying to better himself. It's like, is the glass half full, or is he going to throw the glass at me and accuse me of fucking his friends?

— Rosalie Bahmer

What's brutal about the first date is the scrutiny. When you think about this person in terms of the future, you magnify everything. The guy will be like, "Could I look at uneven eyebrows for the rest of my life?" And the woman is thinking, "Do I want somebody looking at me like this for the rest of my life?"

— Jerry Seinfeld

41

My rules for dating: I don't want to hear about your car, I don't want to hear about your ex-girlfriend, I don't want to hear about your boring-ass job. The most romantic thing you can do is relax, buy me drinks, and shut the hell up.

— Wanda Sykes

Dating is like a box of chocolates, sometimes you get something weird.

— Rosie Tran

I met a guy who said those three little words girls want to hear: "You're not fat."

— Joanne Syrigonakis

How do you tell if a guy is really into you? Before the first time you go over to his apartment, he cleans his bathroom.

— Wendy Wilkins

I went out with one girl who said, "Don't treat me like a date, treat me like you would your mom." So I didn't call her for six months.

— Zorba Jevon

I went out with a guy and after dinner he said, "You're not my type, you're too nice." So I shot him, but in a nice way.

— Ellen Orchid

I was out on a date recently and the guy took me horseback riding. That was kind of fun, until we ran out of quarters.

— Susie Loucks

Going out with a jerky guy is kind of like having a piece of food caught in your teeth. All your friends notice it before you do.

— Livia Squires

I love dating a woman with kids. You learn things. For example, four locks on the bedroom door might seem like overkill, but three is never enough.

— Kelli Dunham

I once dated a kinky investment banker. He insisted on tying me up financially.

— Wendy Kamenoff

On a date I wonder if there is going to be any sex, and if I'm going to be involved.

— Garry Shandling

A man on a date wonders if he'll get lucky. The woman knows.

— Monica Piper

What do you do at the end of a date when you know you don't want to see this person ever again? No matter what you say, it's a lie. "I'll see you around. If you're around, and I'm around, I'll see you around that area. You won't be around me. But you will be around."

— Jerry Seinfeld

I'm still going on bad dates, when by now I should be in a bad marriage.

— Laura Kightlinger

When you first start dating, you have cute nicknames like Honey, Sweetie. A couple of years down the road, it changes to Asshole and Jerkface. You don't mean it, it just happens, like a dysfunctional Wonder Twins. Form of, denial. Shape of, acceptance.

— Joanne Syrigonakis

Dating to me was like this bad game of musical chairs. And the day after I turned twenty-five, the music stopped and the only chairs left were gay, divorced, or had names like Harold and Walter.

— Laurie McDermott

Dating is like driving on the freeway; I can never get to where I'm supposed to be. I know I should to be at the corner of "Engaged to be Married," but instead I'm stuck in the "Valley of Haven't Had an Orgasm for Three Months."

— Christine O'Rourke

College students have something they call "the walk of shame" to describe when a girl has to walk across campus wearing her formal dress from the night before. I say "girl," because guys have a strut of pride. A guy will wake up at 7:00 A.M. on a Sunday and put on a rented tux just to make people think he got some.

— Steve Hofstetter

I'm married now, so I have to do my dating on the Internet.

— Thyra Lees-Smith

Dating is fun, except when her boyfriend comes back from the bathroom and punches me in the face. I was going in for the kill, and so was he.

— Mike Lemme

* DAUGHTERS *

When I was twenty-five, I asked my boss if his daughter was single, and he said, "She's smart, beautiful, and you're not in her league. She wouldn't spit on you!" To which I replied, "Whereas I, sir, would be happy to spit on *you*."

— James Sullivan

I'm not saying that my daughter's new boyfriend is dumb, but he'll fall for the fake stick throw.

— JeanAnn O'Brien

When I was growing up you couldn't blow the horn and the girl comes running out. You had to go to the door. Knock on the door. Tell the parents where you are taking their daughter, what time you're gonna have her home. The parents would always come to the door with a dog behind them the size of a horse. The dog starts sniffing your crotch. Now the dog is raising you off the ground. Pretty soon you want to say, "The heck with your daughter, how much do you want for the dog?"

— Tom Dreesen

My favorite thing to do on a date is go to dinner. Or should I say, have somebody else pay for my food.

— Rebecca Nell

I went out to dinner with a Marine. He looked across the table and he goes, "I could kill you in seven seconds." I go, "I'll just have toast then."

— Margaret Smith

Why is it whenever you go out to dinner with someone you'd really like to impress, you leave the bathroom with a little piece of toilet paper still stuck to your tongue?

— Laura Kightlinger

I went out with this one guy, I was very excited about it. He took me out to dinner, he made me laugh, he made me pay. He's like, "Oh, I'm sorry. I forgot my wallet." "Really? I forgot my vagina."

— Lisa Sunstedt

I can't go out to eat with my current girlfriend. I live on fast food, and she thinks brown rice and tree bark are great sandwich fixings.

— Kelli Dunham

* DIVORCE *

I never even believed in divorce until after I got married.

— Diane Ford

There's a special feeling between divorced people. It's called hate.

— Ellen Orchid

My wife left me. I should have seen it coming, for the past year she called me her insignificant other. By the end of the marriage her favorite position was man on top, woman visiting her mother.

— Daniel Liebert

I'm divorced. I miss my husband, but I'm getting to be a better shot.

— Sheila Kay

I'm twenty-three and divorced. Maybe I should stop making important decisions with a Magic 8 Ball.

— Christina Irene

Why do divorce lawyers run full-page ads on the back of the phone book? I wasn't even thinking about divorce until I got that coupon for fifty percent off.

— Jason Love

When it comes to divorce, absence may not make the heart grow fonder, but it sure cuts down on the gunplay.

— Eileen Courtney

It bothers me that my ex-wife and I still live together, on the same planet.

— Daniel Liebert

I've been divorced for seven years now. Each year I celebrate the anniversary of my divorce by watching my wedding video, backwards. It's very therapeutic. First, you see the bouquet flying into my hands, we take the rings off, we look at each other and say, "Do I?" and march back up the aisle.

— Ellen Orchid

It's hard to talk to divorced men, always sensitive from the divorce. They take things the wrong way. "Nice day, don't you think?" "I don't want to make a commitment." "Want half of my ice cream?" "I don't want half of anything anymore."

— Elayne Boosler

The doctor enters the examination room and says, "OK, lay down. I say, "Buy me a drink first, pig."

— **Judy Tenuta**

* DOGS *

Can you imagine if there were dating services for dogs? I'm thinking my dog's personal ad would read something like this, "Hi, I'm Oliver. My hobbies include digging through the garbage and chewing on pens. I'm seeking a bitch with similar interests, breed unimportant."

— **Andi Rhoads**

Dogs make better companions than men because they don't care which CDs they get in the breakup, and you can blow off their birthday and they'll still lick you.

— **Debbie Kasper**

I've heard that dogs are man's best friend. That explains where men are getting their hygiene tips.

— **Kelly Maguire**

Guys are like dogs. They keep comin' back. Ladies are like cats. Yell at a cat one time, they're gone.

— **Lenny Bruce**

Get two women together, one will say, "Men are dogs." Men are not dogs, because you can trust dogs. I never found panties in my dog's car. My dog never ran up my phone bill calling nine hundred numbers to talk dirty to some nasty ho. My dog doesn't have another family across town he's hiding. Dogs are loyal, they protect you, and they can lick their own balls.

— **Wanda Sykes**

I just got a new dog, Sammy. He's my fourth Beagle. I get about fourteen or fifteen years out of a beagle. I've been married three times and I never get more than ten years out of a husband. I get a lot more mileage out of a beagle than a husband, and if the dogs want to go out and run around, I can have 'em neutered.

— **Meg Maly**

Barbie recently celebrated her fortieth anniversary. If only real women were shown the same respect. Barbie turns forty and she's a collectors' item. A real woman turns forty and she's replaced by Skipper.

— Jennifer Vally

There's this huge variety of Barbie dolls. They have Fun Time Barbie, Aviation Barbie. Oh, get this one: Gift-Giving Ken. You know, I really don't think this is going to prepare my niece for adult relationships. How about Date-Breaking Ken, I-Still-Live-with-My-Mother Ken, and Oh-You-Don't-Mind-If-My-Friend-Bob-Joins-Us Ken?

— Cathy Ladman

Barbie and Ken are still a couple. This proves one thing: you don't need a penis to get a girl, just a really nice convertible.

— Jennifer Vally

They've come up with a new Ken doll. They've made his eyes sparkle, so at least it looks as if he's interested in what Barbie's saying.

— Charisse Savarin

* DOUBLE STANDARDS *

There's a double standard, even today. A man can sleep around and sleep around, and nobody asks any questions. A woman, you make nineteen or twenty mistakes, right away you're a tramp.

— Joan Rivers

* DRESSING *

Men don't feel the urge to get married as quickly as women do because their clothes all button and zip in the front. Women's dresses usually button and zip in the back. We need men emotionally and sexually, but we also need men to help us get dressed.

— Rita Rudner

* DRINKING *

Young guys love to get wasted. Don't! It makes you impotent. Being with a young hottie who can't get it up is like ordering a banana split with all nuts and no banana.

— Elaine Pelino

I can't think of anything worse after a night of drinking, than waking up next to someone and not being able to remember their name, or how you met, or why they're dead.

— *Laura Kightlinger*

I like my men like I like my Pop-Tarts. Toasted.

— *Christina Irene*

* DRIVING *

I'm nervous. This morning my girlfriend got into the car and called shotgun wedding.

— *Craig Sharf*

Always let your spouse get their way when you're talking directions in the car. If they're right, you get where you're going; and if they're wrong, you can blame them the rest of the day. Best case scenario, you can turn around and go home. It's a win-win situation.

— *Jason Love*

When my husband and I are in the car, I usually let him drive. Because when I drive, he has a tendency to bite the dashboard.

— **Rita Rudner**

My husband doesn't like my driving. How did I know he was standing behind my car in the driveway?

— **Mary Pfeiffer**

* **EMOTIONS** *

Men only have two feelings, we're either hungry or horny. I tell my wife, if I don't have an erection, make me a sandwich.

— **Bobby Slayton**

Men and women have always had problems relating. As children, men were told: "Be a man. Don't cry!" and women were told, "Let it out. Cry, you'll feel better!" And that's why as adults, women become very emotional, and men become snipers.

— **Pam Stone**

Women get their heart broke, they cry. Men don't do that. Men hold it in like it don't hurt. They walk around and get hit by trucks. "Didn't he see that truck?" "Man, he wouldn't have seen a 747. His heart was broke."

— *Richard Pryor*

Share your feelings with your woman. And she'll leave you for a guy who never cries and who spanks her.

— *Jim Carrey*

I'm not afraid to reveal my deepest feelings to a woman, "I love bacon! I hate tight underpants! Yankees ain't gotta chance this year, not with that pitching!"

— *Daniel Liebert*

* ENGAGEMENT RINGS *

Many of my friends are getting engaged and are buying diamonds for their fiancée. What better to symbolize marriage than the hardest thing known to man.

— *Mike Dugan*

It's amazing what we pay for diamonds. They're just rocks. Who decided that the diamond was going to be the engagement rock? In a different world, I might have paid four grand for limestone.

— *Jeff Scott*

That night is the most romantic we guys get. I remember when I asked my wife to marry me, I got down on my knee and I was shaking a little stick and I went, "Ooops, that's not the color we're looking for is it, honey?" I get teary-eyed just thinking about it.

— Jack Coen

When my fiancé proposed it was very romantic. He turned off the TV. Well, he muted it. During the commercial.

— Wendy Liebman

I was engaged once when I was twenty-three, but I had to call it off. It turned out I wasn't pregnant after all.

— Frances Dilorinzo

Being engaged sucks. I was engaged for a year. If dating is like shopping, being engaged is like having a guy put you on lay-a-way. Like saying, "I know I want it. I just want to delay taking it home as long as possible."

— Kris McGaha

Engaged women have sex 2.9 times a week. And the .9 is really frustrating.

— Jay Leno

Before we got engaged he never farted. Now it's a second language.

— Caroline Rhea

It's amazing how many beautiful women walk into your life the week before you get married.

— Jason Love

I had a nasty engagement that gave me pre-divorce jitters.

— Bonnie Cheeseman

* EXERCISE *

Married people don't have to exercise, because our attitude is: "They've seen us naked already, and they like it."

— Carol Montgomery

My wife is now doing Pilates. I think that's his name.

— Peter Sasso

* EX-HUSBANDS *

My ex-husband threatened to commit suicide if I left him. Which is so sad, because if he'd killed himself I probably would have stayed.

— *Charisse Savarin*

Never bad-mouth your ex-husband to your kids. Because if you do, then you ruin the moment when they figure it out all by themselves.

— *Cory Kahaney*

I hear my ex-husband is dating someone. I don't know anything about her, except she's perfect for him, because she's not me.

— *Wendy Kamenoff*

My ex-husband was a drummer, and he had this nervous habit of hitting on things, like my girlfriends. Yeah, he was always banging on something.

— *LeMaire*

I call my ex-husband by the last name I knew him, Plaintiff.

— JeanAnn O'Brien

* FANTASIES *

I'm a modern woman; most of my fantasies are of more sleep.

— Laura Hayden

What's the number-one fantasy for most guys? Two women. Fellows, I think that's a bit lofty. Come on, if you can't satisfy that one woman, why you want to piss off another one? Why have two angry women in bed with you at the same time?

— Wanda Sykes

My husband wanted to spice up our love life with role play. He said, "I'll fulfill your fantasy if you fulfill mine." I said, "Great. Me first: clean the bathtub."

— Stephanie Blum

My biggest sex fantasy is we're making love and I realize I'm out of debt.

— Beth Lapides

* FLIRTING *

My biggest problem with dating is that I have no game. Some women can just bat their eyes and men come running. The men just keep popping up one after another. It's like they have a magical man-filled Pez dispenser.

— Lori Giarnella

* FOOTBALL *

I've been trying to understand men by watching football, and I noticed that they treat the football like a woman. They hold on to it, they take it places and never let it out of their sight. Until the moment they score, when they toss it aside.

— Maureen Murphy

A poll shows women think men are sexiest playing football. And they're at their least sexy watching football.

— Jay Leno

My husband is from England, and has never seen a football game before. So I could tell him anything I wanted. I told him it was over at half time.

— Rita Rudner

* FOREPLAY *

Women prefer thirty to forty minutes of foreplay. Men prefer thirty to forty seconds of foreplay. Men consider driving back to her place as part of the foreplay.

— Matt Groening

Men keep rushing through lovemaking. Which is the part I like, the beginning part. Most women are like that. We need time to warm up. Why is this hard for you guys to understand? You are the first people to tell us not to gun a cold engine. You want us to go from zero to sixty in a minute. We're not built like that. We stall.

— Anita Wise

Married people know that foreplay is when he pushes the mute button on ESPN.

— Dr. Terri

Everybody needs a black friend for truthful advice. A white friend will sugarcoat her advice. "Maybe you need a good makeover. Life isn't about being rich: hang in there sweetie, he'll find a better job." Whereas my black girlfriend will say, "Girl: you ugly. Yo' ass is poor, and you need to take yo' baby's daddy to court for that money."

— Emily Rush

It's difficult to be friends with men. Say hi to a guy, and he thinks you want him. I said hello to my neighbor and heard him tell a friend, "That's my girlfriend!" I was so mad! And not just because he was five years old. That's so arrogant.

— Roberta Rockwell

Women, don't introduce your boyfriend to your girlfriends. We will hate all of them, except the two we will try to get with after you and I break up.

— Mike Lemme

* FUNERALS *

I know one woman who had her husband cremated, and then mixed his ashes with grass and smoked him. She said, "That's the best he's made me feel for years."

— Maureen Murphy

* GAY *

I had a hard time telling my parents I'm gay, so I broke the news to them gradually: I told them I wasn't gay, but the woman I was sleeping with was.

— E. L. Greggory

* GAY MARRIAGE *

My parents were worried about me getting married, so I got married. But they have a problem with it: she's black. But she's also doctor, so it's okay.

— Marla Lukofsky

I'm in favor of gay marriage. Then at least both people are excited about planning the wedding.

— Jay Leno

I was once involved in a same-sex marriage. There was the same sex over and over and over.

— David Letterman

I'm against gay marriage. I think marriage is a sacred union between a man and a pregnant woman.

— Craig Kilborn

Canada said, "We'll see your legalization of sodomy and raise you gay marriage." But here in the U.S. marriage is a sacred act between two people chosen by a studio audience.

— Jon Stewart

Congratulations, gay people! You are about to discover the joys of alimony.

— Craig Ferguson

* GIFTS *

I know my girlfriend thinks I'm weird, because sometimes she says thank you, but with a question mark. Like the other day, when I gave her a birthday present. "What is this, a refrigerator door? *Thank you?*"

— Geoff Holtzman

For my thirty-first birthday, my boyfriend bought me a treadmill. He's dead now. So young, so tragic, so clueless.

— Mel Fine

Not romantic, my husband. Do you know what he gave me for Mother's Day? A George Foreman grill. I gave it back to him for Father's Day, in a sort of forceful upward motion.

— Sandi Selvi

* GIRLFRIENDS *

My girlfriend is a remote control freak. She takes it with her everywhere she goes.

— Craig Sharf

My girlfriend's weird. One day she asked me, "If you could know how and when you were going to die, would you want to know?" I said, "No." She said, "Okay, forget it."

— Steven Wright

I don't have a girlfriend. But I do know a woman who'd be mad at me for saying that.

— **Mitch Hedberg**

Remember "going with" someone when you were a little girl? When I was in fifth grade, Bucky McGinn came up to me on the playground and asked me to go with him. I said yes. And that was it; I never ever heard from him again. As far as I'm concerned, we're still going. I don't care if he is married with two kids.

— **Mary Gallagher**

I think dating was a lot easier when we were younger. Dating was so much easier when we were younger because we all spoke the same cryptic code and understood the rules of engagement. "Shelly, ask Suzie to ask Mary to ask Mike to ask Billy, if he likes me. But tell her not to let him know that I like him. Well OK, she can tell Billy that I like him, but not that I *like* him, *like* him."

— **Lori Gianella**

I'm seeing a new girl now. She's fantastic. It's mostly through the window.

— **Steve Hofstetter**

* GRANDPARENTS *

I never will forget my granny. One day she's sitting out on the porch and I said, "Granny, how old does a woman get before she don't want no more boyfriends?" She was around 106 then. She said, "I don't know, honey, you'll have to ask somebody older than me."

— Moms Mabley

It's hard to find the right guy, because the example of my grandparent's marriage sets a really high bar. My grandfather escaped from a concentration camp so that he and my grandmother could hide in the forest together. And they went on to be happily married for sixty-seven years. So what do I ask guys on the first date? "Do you like sushi? Would you run from Nazis with me?"

— Janet Rosen

* G-SPOT *

I think the articles in women's magazines are totally unrealistic about what you can expect from a man in bed. I saw this article entitled: "Training your man to find your G-spot." Get real. The guy I'm dating can't even find my apartment.

— Livia Squires

My wife told me of a book about the G-spot. I went to a bookstore, I couldn't even find the book. My wife bought it for me, but there were no pictures, maps, or diagrams. It just said the G-spot was about two-thirds of the way in. Compared to who?

— **Robert Schimmel**

I believe the only time it's appropriate for a man go with the strong belief that he should *not* stop and ask for directions is when he's looking for my G-spot. No, you're not quite there yet, "Maybe veer to the left?" Oh, just keep going, you'll find it!

— **Nancy Patterson**

* GUNS *

This woman goes into a gun shop and says, "I want to buy a gun for my husband." The clerk asks, "Did he tell you what kind of gun?" "No," she replied, "He doesn't even know I'm going to shoot him."

— **Phyllis Diller**

* GYMNASTICS *

I competed in gymnastics, but I learned never to tell guys I'm dating that I was a gymnast. They think they hit the sexual lottery. But gymnasts aren't necessarily wild in bed, we're just normal women, who afterwards need to be judged.

— Roberta Rockwell

* GYMS *

I really get irritated when guys try to hit on me at the gym by telling me how to use the equipment. I was working out with weights and this personal trainer asks, "Are you working on your biceps?" "No, I'm practicing my sledge hammer swings for my next serial kill."

— Liisa Mannerkoski

* HAIR *

I prefer balding men. Why would you want to run your hands through a man's hair, when you could shove your fist right into his skull?

— Stephanie Hodge

I love a man with a mustache. And fortunately for
me, I've found a man who loves a woman with one.

— *Aurora Cotsbeck*

* HAPPINESS *

I'm happiest when my wife gets her way, or so she
tells me.

— *Jason Love*

* HARASSMENT *

Yet another obnoxious attempt by men to try to get
your attention: they hiss. "Sssss! Sssss!" But I like to
think of it as the sound of their ego deflating as I continue to walk away.

— *Mimi Gonzalez*

I hate when I have to walk down the street past construction workers and they always say something disgusting. It wouldn't bother me so much if they could show me even one marriage that came from this kind of introduction. "Mommy, how did you meet Daddy?" "Well, I was walking along the street one day, and your father screamed something about wanting to eat his lunch off my ass. I was so turned on, I threw myself in the back of his truck."

— Caroline Rhea

* HEALTH SUPPLEMENTS *

How do vitamins know where to go? A is supposed to help the eyes, E the heart, do they have a map? I take them, but I don't feel better. But I guess when you take your vitamins with vodka, they get tipsy and confused, lose the map and go straight to my breasts. Like most guys after a couple drinks.

— Jayne Warren

* HEIGHT *

I like to date short guys, because us women love anything we can throw into our purse. "Let's see, keys, lipstick—oh I forgot I was dating you, and you've eaten all my Altoids."

— LeMaire

Short guys are always staying stupid things to me because I'm so tall. One guy asked, "Do you play basketball?" I said, "No, do you play miniature golf?"

— Frances Dilorinzo

I'm 4'11" and I've learned why tall guys date short girls: we're the only one who can fit through the sunroof if they lock the keys in the car.

— Robin Fairbanks

Being a tall woman, I always dated guys for their height rather than their wealth, because I wasn't thinking.

— Frances Dilorinzo

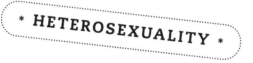

* HETEROSEXUALITY *

You're born a heterosexual. It's not a choice. Who would choose this? The guilt, the shame...and do you think I'm *happy* having to hire a decorator?

— Garry Shandling

In college I experimented with heterosexuality: I slept with a straight guy. I was really drunk.

— Bob Smith

* HOBBIES *

I've been working out lately, it's my new hobby. I thought I already had a hobby, but apparently going out, getting stinking drunk, and giving creepy guys phony phone numbers is not actually considered a hobby, but a "life-style."

— Andi Rhoads

* HOLIDAYS *

Women get a little more excited about New Year's Eve than men do. It's like an excuse, you get drunk, you make a lot of promises you're not going to keep, the next morning as soon as you wake up, you start breaking them. For men, we just call that a date.

— Jay Leno

Valentine's Day blows. It's just another day for you to wake up late, wonder how you're going to pay rent, spend the day sulking in your underwear and a cute tee shirt, eat a goober grape sandwich, and half-assedly clean your apartment. Did I say "you"? Sorry, I meant me.

— Jessica Delfino

Valentine's is a big day for married people. A lot of anticipation. One of the three days you get laid: Valentine's Day, Christmas, your birthday—maybe.

— Aisha Tyler

I wanted to make it really special on Valentines' Day, so I tied my boyfriend up. And for three solid hours I watched whatever I wanted to on TV.

— Tracy Smith

A Valentine's Day survey found 39% of women say a man doesn't have to pay for the dinner. It all depends on how comfortable he is with masturbation.

— Conan O'Brien

Hallmark is coming out with a new card for guys who forget Valentine's Day. The card is small and gold and maxes out at ten grand.

— Craig Kilborn

I don't understand why Cupid was chosen to represent Valentine's Day. When I think about romance, the last thing on my mind is a short, chubby toddler coming at me with a weapon.

— Paul McGinty

* HOME DECOR *

My husband and I are in what some call the "nesting" stage of marriage. Others refer to it as "The Running of the Visa," or "The Sex is Getting Boring, Let's Buy Furniture."

— Christine Blackburn

After seven years of marriage, I'm sure of two things: first, never wallpaper together; and second, you'll need two bathrooms, both for her.

— Dennis Miller

* HOMOSEXUALITY *

My boyfriend and I saw two guys holding hands, and he completely freaked. "That's gross! I'd never do anything like that. That's immoral." But if I were to show him a picture of two naked women together, this is how he thinks, "What's missing? Me!"

— Felicia Michaels

My brother is gay and my parents don't care, as long as he marries a doctor.

— Elayne Boosler

My aunt asked me, "You're a homosexual? Are you seeing a psychiatrist?" "No," I said, "I'm seeing a lieutenant in the army."

— Bob Smith

Next to hot chicken soup, a tattoo of an anchor on your chest, and penicillin, I consider a honeymoon one of the most overrated events in the world.

— Erma Bombeck

Honeymoon night was hot. She was moaning all night in ecstasy, opening gifts. "An orange squeezer! Oh my God! A waffle maker!" Next morning the guy down the hall gave me the big thumbs-up. "Boy, you were using everything but the kitchen sink in there."

— Mike Binder

You might be a redneck, if your honeymoon was featured on *True Stories of the Highway Patrol*.

— Jeff Foxworthy

I was taking caring of myself before I got married, my husband was taking care of himself. I thought, let's just continue down this path. But he would come home and say stuff to like, "What's for dinner?" I reply, "I don't know. What did you cook?" And he actually said this one time, "I'm all out of clean underwear." To which I replied, "Ooh, then you need to wash. I did my laundry yesterday. I got a drawer full of clean panties. You're welcome to borrow a pair to tide you over."

— Wanda Sykes

Living together, it's like I'm a prostitute for really low wages. "I'll do oral and anal, if you take out the garbage."

— Margaret Cho

I love it when my husband thinks I might leave him. He gets so insecure, he does the dishes. But I'd have to file divorce papers to get him to clean the toilet.

— Shirley Lipner

My husband is Muslim, and he prays five times a day. I said, "Sweetie, you're already down on your knees, could you pick up the socks you left under the sofa? And look—the vacuum cleaner is facing Mecca."

— Fiona Walsh

Don't cook. Don't clean. No man will ever make love to a woman because she waxed the linoleum. "My God, the floor's immaculate. Lie down, you hot bitch."

— Joan Rivers

My mom suggested I call the company "Hire a Hubby" to help me around the house. Why? So he can lie around on the couch all day with the husband I already have for free?

— Laurie McDermott

* HOUSING *

The other day I saw a truck carrying a house, and I thought, "That must have been a really nasty divorce." Yeah, as the wife drives away she's scream-ing, "I told you I was going to take the house!" And the husband is shouting, "I'm keeping the basement!"

— Tim Homayoon

* HUMOR *

When a man says he wants to meet a girl with a sense of humor, he means one who will laugh at everything he says while her breasts jiggle.

— Cheri Oteri

Women claim that what they look for in a man is a sense of humor, but I don't believe it. Who do you want removing your bra: Russell Crowe or the Three Stooges?

— Bruce Smirnoff

* HUSBANDS *

I want to get married but I look at husbands the same way I look at tattoos. I want one, but I can't decide what I want, and I don't want to be stuck with something I'd grow to hate and have surgically removed. Why can't I just have a henna husband?

— Margaret Cho

When I get married, I want a regular husband. I don't want a soul mate, because eventually husbands and wives start to hate each other. And when you think about it, a husband is only until "death do you part." But a soul mate is going to harass you for all eternity.

— Livia Squires

When you are looking for a husband, it's important to find someone with a good sense of humor, a good lover, someone who likes to do housework, and someone who has lots of money. Just make sure that these four men never meet.

— Meg Maly

He tricked me into marrying him. He told me he was pregnant.

— Carol Leifer

My husband and I are totally different. My friends always try to make me feel better by saying "opposites attract." I guess that's true because he was a virgin, and I...

— Frances Dilorinzo

My husband is a rock musician, and never had a day job. So when we first met he thought I had an obsessive compulsive disorder because every single morning, I'd go to work.

— Roberta Rockwell

My husband and I used to fight about that night out with the guys, but it's not like I was doing it every night.

— Jenny Jones

When I was sixteen years old, I dated my husband for about a month before I dumped him. Then when I was eighteen, I dated him again for three months before I broke up with him, because I thought it wasn't going anywhere. When I was twenty-eight, I married him. I was thinking, "If I dump him this time, I get to keep his stuff."

— Frances Dilorinzo

The only thing my husband and I have in common is that we were married on the same day.

— Phyllis Diller

They think it's your destiny to clean, and I guess it's their destiny to have a couch surgically implanted on their behind. You may marry the man of your dreams ladies, but years later you're married to a couch that burps.

— Roseanne Barr

I've been married a while. You know you've become too dependent on your husband when you ask him to scratch an itch you can reach yourself.

— Roberta Rockwell

Does your husband sit around the house in his shorts, fart and drink beer and watch football? All right! I do that, too. My new husband tells me that's not very ladylike. I say, "Neither is a blow job, and you don't complain about that." Which pretty much ends that conversation.

— Diane Ford

My husband was an animal in bed. A ferret.

— Wendy Liebman

My husband is so quiet, I've collected life insurance on him twice.

— Jean Carroll

Husbands think we should know where everything is, like the uterus is a tracking device. He asks me, "Roseanne, do we have any Cheetos left?" Like he can't go over to that sofa cushion and lift it himself.

— Roseanne Barr

He was cheating on me with his secretary. I found lipstick on his collar, covered with White-Out.

— Wendy Liebman

My, that man was ugly. My husband was so ugly he hurt my feelings.

— Moms Mabley

My husband said he needed more space. So I locked him outside.

— Roseanne Barr

* INSECTS *

I was reading how a female spider will eat the male spider after mating. I guess female spiders know that life insurance is easier to collect than child support.

— Janine DiTullio

* INSURANCE *

My wife and I took out life insurance policies on one another, so now it's just a waiting game.

— Bil Dwyer

Many married couples have high life insurance policies. That's why they fly in separate planes to the same place; in case one crashes, the other wins the lottery.

— Laurie McDermott

* INTERNET *

I have so much cyber sex, my baby's first words will be: "You've got mail."

— *Paulara R. Hawkins*

* INTIMACY *

My last date told me I had a fear of intimacy. I said, "Hey, I let you in the house, didn't I?"

— *Michele Balan*

* JEALOUSY *

It's stupid to be jealous of your partner's past. That's none of your business. I know Lisa had sex before we met. I can handle that. Of course, she didn't enjoy it.

— *Rick Reynolds*

Men get jealous more often, but when women do, they go demented sometimes, and for weird reasons. I never thought that until I got married, and one day my wife came home from work and was mad at me, because there was a pretty woman on the bus she thought I would have liked, "You bastard, you're horrible!"

— Ray Romano

Jealousy has the "lousy" built right into it.

— Jason Love

* JOBS *

Women need to like the job of the guy they're with. Men, if they are physically attracted to a woman, are not that concerned with her job. "Slaughterhouse? You're just lopping their heads off? Great! Why don't you shower, and we'll get some burgers."

— Jerry Seinfeld

* KISSING *

Everyone remembers their first kiss. My first kiss, for example—I'm looking forward to remembering it.

— Matze Knop

First dates are always so awkward. I find myself thinking, "Is it too soon for a kiss? No, I can do this, why not? Oh my God, that's my tongue! Why are there suddenly tongues involved? Okay, I need to stop now, I need to slow down, this is getting too heated, too fast. Whatever happens, I need to keep my clothes on, and my hands out of his pants, because it's too soon, and other people in the restaurant are trying to eat."

— Lori Chapman

Someone asked me the other day, "When was the last time you kissed someone?" and I replied, "Does licking a postage stamp count?"

— Sandy Ehlers

* LESBIANISM *

You know, my family always said no man would be good enough for me.

— Suzy Berger

Introductions are tricky in a lesbian relationship. It's a word game. To my friends she's my lover, to strangers and family members in denial she's my roommate, to Jehovah's Witnesses at the door she's my lesbian sex slave, and to my mother she's Jewish, and that's all that matters.

— Denise McCanles

Heterosexuals are rude sometimes, get right in your face and ask you rude questions, "What do you lesbians do in bed?" Well, it's a lot like heterosexual sex. Only, one of us doesn't have to fake an orgasm.

— Suzanne Westenhoefer

My mother always told me, "Marry someone like your father." I knew I was a dyke, but to this day I'm so set on pleasing my mother that I now find myself attracted to women who are balding and have a beer belly.

— Monica Grant

* LINES *

Meeting guys is hard. I read in *Cosmo* that a good icebreaker is to tell men that they resemble a celebrity. So I went up to this one guy and said, "Wow, you look just like Urkel." He muttered something in Chinese and ran away.

— Andrea Henry

Guys I've been meeting have the worst pickup lines. Like, "Hey, what's your friend's name?"

— Melanie Reno

I hate bars. Guys come up to me and say, "Hey, cupcake, can I buy you a drink?" I say, "No, but I'll take the six bucks."

— Margaret Smith

Men use this line after a date, "Let's go home and cuddle." What they don't say is what they want you to cuddle with.

— Stacey Prussman

At the end of the date this guy pulled out the oldest line, "Hey, baby how about breakfast? Should I call you or nudge you?" I said, "Write me."

— Diane Nichols

* LINGERIE *

When do we put on the lingerie? Always at the beginning of the relationship, right? First couple of months, you know, strutting around the bedroom wearing a teddy. Six months later, you've stopped shaving your legs and you look like a teddy.

— Carol Leifer

* LIVING TOGETHER *

My boyfriend and I just moved in together to see if we're compatible enough for marriage. It's like we're leasing a car with the option to buy.

— Stacey Prussman

My girlfriend and I decided to live together instead of getting married. We get the all benefits of marriage without a wedding ceremony, which means we'll grow to hate each other but won't have any free stuff to show for it.

— Steve Boyer

My wife wouldn't live with me before we were married. Now that we've been married for fifteen years I'm trying to talk her into getting her own place again.

— Jeffrey Jena

* LONGEVITY *

I was performing at Atlantic City and I asked this lady in the audience how long she'd been married. She said, "Forty-one years." I said, "That's amazing. How did you do it?" And she said, "I wouldn't recommend it."

— Jane Condon

My parents have been married for fifty-five years. The secret to their longevity? "Outlasting your opponent."

— **Cathy Ladman**

They say married men live longer. It just seems longer.

— **Bobby Slayton**

My parents stayed together for forty years, but that was out of spite.

— **Woody Allen**

My mom had good advice for me about how to stay married for a long time. She said, "Always remember, honesty is very important. It must be avoided. And the most important thing is, you have to let your husband be himself, and you have to pretend he's someone else."

— **Rita Rudner**

* LOOKS *

I don't date good-looking guys, mainly because they don't ask. But ugly guys are *sooo* grateful, they'll give you anything. I have two kidneys in a bottle, just in case.

— **Joanne Syrigonakis**

There are a lot of good-looking men out there. But keep in mind that no matter how cute and sexy a guy is, there's always some woman somewhere who is sick of him.

— Carol Henry

There's no leeway for a woman's looks. You never see a man walking down the street with a woman who has a little potbelly and a bald spot

— Elayne Boosler

Women look in a mirror, and no matter what they look like in real life, they always think they look worse. Guys look in a mirror and think they look substantially better than they are. No matter how much of a three-toed, knuckle-dragger a guy is, he figures he's four or five sit-ups away from being in the hot tub with Elle McPherson.

— Richard Jeni

* LOVE *

I fall in love really quickly and this scares guys away. I'm like, "I'm in love with you, I want to marry you, I want to move in with you.'" And they're like, "Ma'am, could you give me the ten bucks for the pizza, and I'll be outta here."

— Penny Wiggins

I fall in love all the time. I'm accident prone.

— Mari Lund

Love is the answer, but while you're waiting for the answer, sex raises some pretty good questions.

— Woody Allen

If you open your heart up, and let all the love you have flow out of you, I promise that some highly-dysfunctional, emotionally-unavailable man will glom himself onto you and never let go.

— Wendy Kamenoff

When you're in love, it's the most glorious two and a half days of your life.

— Richard Lewis

If it is your time, love will track you down like a cruise missile.

— Lynda Barry

Once I thought I was in love. Then I realized it was just gas.

— Wendy Wilkins

Love is blind. I guess that's why it proceeds by the sense of touch.

— Morey Amsterdam

Before I met my husband I'd never fallen in love, though I've stepped in it a few times.

— Rita Rudner

Don't you hate it when you date someone and they say this, "I love you, but I'm not *in* love with you." You just want to go, "I want you, but not inside me."

— Felicia Michaels

I am certainly not an authority on love because there are no authorities on love, just those who've had luck with it, and those who haven't.

— **Bill Cosby**

George was my first love. He was the one I lost my virginity to the first time.

— **JeanAnn O'Brien**

I urge you all to love yourselves without reservation, and to love each other without restraints. Unless you're into leather. Then, by all means, use restraints.

— **Margaret Cho**

Is Cupid blind or just sadistic?

— **Jason Love**

Love for me has always been like a pretzel. Twisted and salty.

— **Emmy Gay**

A poll showed that two out of five men would rather have love than money or health. Yeah, that's what a woman wants: a broke, sick guy.

— **Jay Leno**

My love life is like a fairy tale. Grimm.

— **Wendy Liebman**

They say, "If you have true love, let it go and it will come back." I don't think so. True love is like a cupcake; it should be enjoyed immediately.

— Vinny Badabing

Love is a feeling you feel when you're about to feel a feeling you never felt before.

— Flip Wilson

I know I'm really in love when I imagine how sad I would be if he died, and what I would wear to the funeral.

— Tamara Pennington

Being in love is like having Multiple Personality Disorder. You can never make up your mind. "Come here, baby. Get the hell away from me! Let me hold you. You prick! I love you. Where are you going? Come back!" Just call me Sybil.

— Mike Cotayo

A lot of people wonder how you know if you're really in love. Just ask yourself this one question: "Would I mind being financially destroyed by this person?"

— **Ronnie Shakes**

Love is like playing checkers. You have to know which man to move.

— **Moms Mabley**

Love is staying awake all night with a sick child. Or a very healthy adult.

— **David Frost**

I feel if I'm lucky, I'll fall in love. If I'm unlucky, I'll fall and hit my head.

— **Emmy Gay**

I was in love once, but I couldn't stay with someone that self-centered. There are more important things to worry about in the world...like me.

— **Rosie Tran**

The difference between love and sex is that sex relieves tension and love causes it.

— **Woody Allen**

There's a fine line between true love and a stalking conviction.

— **Buzz Nutley**

It took me until I was thirty-three to fall in love. But I knew that was going to happen, because in college I wasn't the girl who got the booty call, I got called to help them move a couch.

— *Wendy Wilkins*

Ah, those three magic words. You want to start a fight, ask a man this question: "Do you love me?" "Ah fuck, here we go. I told you a long time ago. When you got that income tax check. Not the state, the federal. Memmer?" "But do you love me?" "I'm here, ain't I? All my tools are at your mom's house. You cosigned on the truck. Where am I going?"

— *George Lopez*

You have heard the adage, "You can't love another, until you can love yourself." I disagree. It may be difficult to enter into a healthy relationship whilst marinating in a quagmire of self-loathing. But it is a mere can of corn to devote twenty-three hours a day to obsessing over someone who is only vaguely aware that you borrowed the Metro section of his newspaper at Starbucks.

— *Janeane Garofalo*

There are couples who kill themselves for love, like Romeo and Juliet. But how do you bring that up on a date? What if she's not ready yet? You have to be real slick, say something like, "Want to shoot some pool, then each other? Maybe we can tie the knot, and kick the chair out from underneath?"

— *Steve Hofstetter*

I hate first dates. I made the mistake of telling my date a lie about myself and she caught me. I didn't think she'd actually demand to see the Bat Cave.

— Alex Reed

Men like to lie. I met this guy on the Internet. He said he lives in a big house, hundreds of rooms, basketball court, and a big yard. I was ready to marry the dude, until I found out he was on Death Row. Men like to lie.

— Leah Eva

If a man lies to you, don't get mad, get even. I once dated a guy who waited three months into our relationship before he told me he was married. I said, "Hey, don't worry about it. I used to be a man."

— Livia Squires

I've got my own lie detector at home. I call her "honey."

— Jason Love

Everybody lies about sex. People lie during sex. If it weren't for lies, there'd be no sex.

— Jerry Seinfeld

It's hard to trust when dating through personal ads. To make the personals more truthful, I think there should be a Pinocchio effect. Whenever a guy lies, his nose would grow. No, better yet, his member would shrink. This would cut down on both the betrayal and the birth rate.

— Caryl Fuller

You can never trust the descriptions you get of someone you meet on the Internet. After all, that's what email stands for: "Embellished Measurements and Incredible Lies."

— Robert Murray

I used to date a girl who was a terrible liar. I could read her like a book. Unfortunately, it was a porno mag, which said a lot about our relationship.

— Jonathan Bell

* MAGAZINES *

My old boyfriend used to say, "I read *Playboy* for the articles." Right, and I go to shopping malls for the music.

— Rita Rudner

A lot of women write into magazines with these really petty complaints about men, like "He spends too much time with his friends" or "I think he might be cheating on me." Folks, I've been in some bad relationships before. Don't complain to me about men until you've been shot at.

— Livia Squires

Women reading *Vogue* magazine about the latest fashions to come off the Paris runway, is the same as men looking at naked women in *Playboy*. We're both looking at places we're never going to visit.

— Andi Rhoads

* MANNERS *

Men have hidden agendas. For instance, every time a man holds the door open for me, I think he's just doing it to check out my ass. Or at least I hope so.

— Stacey Prussman

* MARRIAGE *

I'm not interested in marriage. But everyone always asks, "Don't you want to meet that special guy?" Hey, I meet special guys all the time. And if I was married, I'd have to stop doing that.

— Lee Arleth

My take on marriage is this: why buy the butcher when you can get the sausage for free?

— Jen Kerwin

I don't want to get married because I don't like the idea of sharing income with a guy. I mean, I don't make that much money as it is, and I need all of it for gambling.

— Courtney Cronin

I'm not married. I hope to be someday so I can stop exercising.

— Jeff Stilson

I've never been married. I'd like to find that special someone I can grow old with. Someone I can nurture. Someone who can straighten out my finances.

— Mike Dugan

My momma told me that a man only needed four seasons to make up his mind about marriage. "If he hasn't made up his mind to marry you in a year, you're not getting any younger, and he'll only get lazier."

— Emily Rush

Whenever anyone in our family announces that they're getting married, my first thought is: "How many months along is she?"

— Wendy Wilkins

I think the bottom line difference between being single and being married is this: when you're single you're as happy as you are. When you're married, you can only be as happy as the least happy person in the apartment.

— Tom Hertz

You know what I did before I married? Anything I wanted to.

— Henny Youngman

A friend gave me some advice when I was engaged, "Benefit from my knowledge and mistakes," she said. "When you're married, expect to give some things up. Like dating."

— Roberta Rockwell

Why did I get married? Well, I wasn't getting any sex, and I wasn't making a woman happy, so I figured: why not make it official?

— The Covert Comic

Marriage is what happens when two people's fears are compatible.

— Denise Munro Robb

As soon as you say "I do," you'll discover that marriage is like a car. Both of you might be sitting in the front seat, but only one of you is driving. And most marriages are more like a motorcycle than a car. Somebody has to sit in the back, and you have to yell just to be heard.

— *Wanda Sykes*

Every time I tell someone I'm newly married, they say, "Ohhhh, you're married?" I can hear them thinking, "You're screwed now!"

— *Laurie McDermott*

We've been married three months. I'm just not used to being wrong so often.

— *Dennis Regan*

Being happily married is like having a shit job with people you dig.

— *Jack Coen*

I love being married. It's so great to find that one special person you want to annoy for the rest of your life.

— *Rita Rudner*

Maybe I'm an old-fashioned guy, but I believe the most important thing in a marriage is me.

— *Daniel Liebert*

Don't make any major decisions when you first get married. Your love is so fresh and new, it's hypnotizing. You'll agree to anything. I was like, "Sure, we can live with your parents!"

— *Roberta Rockwell*

Marriage is just legalized laundry and a comfort level with farting you never thought you'd have.

— *Fiona Walsh*

Marriage is great because you can feel secure in the knowledge that you're always going to have someone to fight with.

— *Janet Rosen*

My wife and I have been married almost a year. The first year's the hardest, and then the second's even harder.

— *Tom Arnold*

Never, ever, discount the idea of marriage. Sure, someone might tell you that marriage is just a piece of paper. Well, so is money, and what's more life-affirming than cold, hard cash?

— *Dennis Miller*

Did you ever notice that the word "marriage" is one vocal inflection away from being "mirage?" Just look at some of the terms we give to this supposedly happy union: "wedlock" sounds like incarceration to me. "Your Better Half," which assumes that you're the fucked-up part of the union.

— Wanda Sykes

I love being married. I was single for a long time, and I just got so sick of finishing my own sentences.

— Brian Kiley

All men make mistakes, but married men find out about them sooner.

— Red Skelton

We were married for better or worse. I couldn't have done better and she couldn't have done worse.

— Henny Youngman

How do people stay together, besides children, real estate, and substance abuse? I think the only solution is to find someone with exactly the same amount of problems as you, like the nuclear deterrence theory from the Cold War. Same amount of problems, but just to keep it interesting, how about a different configuration? For example, "I'll take the career difficulty, she gets the family trauma, and we share the sexual dysfunction." I wrote that before I lived it.

— Norman K.

Marriage is very difficult. Marriage is like a 5,000-piece jigsaw puzzle, all sky.

— Cathy Ladman

I know a man who thinks marriage is a fifty-fifty proposition, which convinces us that he doesn't understand women or percentages.

— Henny Youngman

Let us now set forth one of the fundamental truths about marriage: the wife is in charge.

— Bill Cosby

Now, of course, I realize that a mixed marriage means one between a man and a woman.

— Michael Feldman

Getting married is a lot like getting into a tub of hot water. After you get used to it, it ain't so hot.

— Minnie Pearl

I tell ya, my wife, we get along good because we have our own arrangement. One night a week I go out with the boys and one night a week, she goes out with the boys.

— Rodney Dangerfield

Marriage is not a man's idea. A woman must have thought of it. Years ago some guy said, "Let me get this straight, honey. I can't sleep with anyone else for the rest of my life, and if things don't work out, you get to keep half my stuff? What a great idea."

— Bobby Slayton

Marriage is all about him. What he wants, what he needs. What about what I want, what I need? I need love, I need attention, I need a new BMW.

— Laurie McDermott

There's a study in Maine that found if you marry someone who doesn't appreciate you, tries to control you and always has to be right: you may be unhappy. They also discovered that going without water for long periods of time makes you thirsty.

— Caroline Rhea

People say, "Listening is the key to a successful marriage." Ha. Whenever I listen to what my husband is saying, all I hear is, "It's true, I married an asshole."

— Laurie McDermott

I've been married three years. It's crazy because I didn't think any of my marriages would last this long, much less the first one.

— Bill Blank

Marriage is real tough because you have to deal with feelings, and lawyers.

— Richard Pryor

The problem with marriage is that it involves men and women. And that's a pretty bad match.

— Cathy Ladman

I have a pretty good grip on my relationship; I can sense when something is wrong. Like when I say, "I love you," and my wife comes back with, "Okay." That means I have to re-think everything I've done in the past twenty-four hours.

— Steve Brown

The secret to a successful marriage is doing things. My husband and I, we go see movies, we go to dinner, we go on vacation, and once in awhile we do these things together.

— Laurie McDermott

That married couples can live together day after day is a miracle that the Vatican has overlooked.

— Bill Cosby

They say marriage is a contract. No, it's not. Contracts come with warrantees. When something goes wrong, you can take it back to the manufacturer. If your husband starts acting up, you can't take him back to his mama's house. "I don't know; he just stopped working. He's just laying around making a funny noise."

— Wanda Sykes

Answers to the question "How ya doin'?"
Single guy: "Good!"
Married guy: "Hanging in there."
Married guy with kids: "Don't ask!"

— Rich Feldman

When you're single, you're the dictator of your own life: "I give the order to fall asleep on the sofa in the middle of the day!" When married, you're part of a vast decision-making body, and this is if the marriage works. That's what's so painful about divorce: you get impeached and you're not even the president.

— Jerry Seinfeld

You know your marriage is in trouble when your wife starts wearing the wedding ring on her middle finger.

— Dennis Miller

Know what I missed most at the end of my marriage? Putting my cold feet on the back of his warm legs at night. I used to love that. But then it stopped bothering him, so I quit doing it.

— Diane Ford

I was married for two years. Which is a long time if you break it down into half-hour segments.

— Charisse Savarin

I was married for thirteen years. Unfortunately, my husband was only married for ten.

— JeanAnn O'Brien

* MARRIED SEX *

Sex when you're married is like going to the 7-Eleven: there's not much variety, but at three in the morning, it's always there.

— Carol Leifer

Making love while you're married is like being a bad Little League player. Even if you suck, they still have to put you in for two innings.

— Buzz Nutley

A recent magazine article was titled, "Your Top 15 Questions about Sex." But I know from experience that there are only two questions married people ask about sex: number one, "When are we going to have sex?" Number two: "When are we going to have sex again?" Repeat questions one and two as needed.

— Dr. Terri

A survey asked married women when they most want to have sex. Eighty-four percent of them said right after their husband is finished.

— Jay Leno

You know what's great about married sex? It's comfortable. None of that awkwardness about what goes where, or when, how many minutes for this, how many minutes for that. It's like the old Holiday Inn ad: "Sometimes the best surprise is no surprise at all."

— Dr. Terri

When we got married, I told my wife I like sex twice a day. She said, "Me, too." Now we never see each other.

— Rodney Dangerfield

* MASSAGES *

My husband likes massages. I booked a masseuse to come to the house. Wasn't that a good idea? I thought so, until the doorbell rang, and there was an eighteen-year-old blond girl standing there, saying, "I'm here to give your husband a massage." I said, "He's dead."

— Rita Rudner

* MATCHMAKERS *

I got desperate and went to one of those expensive matchmakers. She was so romantic: "You've got to get a guy on the hook. You reel him in slowly." I asked, "When do I fillet him?" I don't know much more about relationships, but I can run a fish and chips.

— Maura Lake

Here's a tip: don't give your home phone number to that dating service Great Expectations, because they'll call you at 9 P.M. on a Saturday night. "What are you doing home, loser?" Genius marketing, I signed up for a year. But halfway through the conversation, I was like, "Wait a second, what are you doing working on a Saturday night, Miranda?"

— Tamara Pennington

* MEETING *

People always tell me, "Get out there, and you'll meet someone you like." Are they kidding? I can't even meet someone I *don't* like.

— Janet Rosen

I have a lot of friends who are single, and they complain about how hard it is to meet people. I think they're wrong. Meeting people is easy. It's maintaining the intricate web of lies that's tricky.

— Douglas Gale

I'd just like to meet a girl with a head on her shoulders. I hate necks.

— Steve Martin

The best way to meet a man in any town is in your car. If you see a cute one walking, just hit him. It's a great icebreaker, and you get to swap telephone numbers.

— Debbie Kasper

You're never going to meet the perfect person. The timing's off. You're married, she's single. You're a Jew, he's Palestinian. One's a Mexican, one's a raccoon. One's a black man, one's a black woman. It's always something.

— Chris Rock

I was at the grocery store the other day when I saw this really cute brunette. I was about to go and talk to her, maybe ask her out on a date, but when I saw she was buying soy milk, I said to myself, "Nah, I don't think so." I know how it would go: we'd argue about politics, she'd nag me about not recycling, and my current girlfriend would kill me.

— Douglas Gale

Last night I met a guy, and I was wondering, "What would our kids look like, where would we live? Would he get along with my mother?" And then he asked, "Can I take your order?"

— Denise Munro Robb

Where can you find the perfect man? On TV. You see him thirty minutes a week, and his lines are written for him.

— Mary Pfeiffer

Men should be color-coded to save us time, with a dot on their foreheads. So if you see a guy with a red dot it's a red alert, "Red alert! Married, in town on convention, cheater!" A yellow dot would indicate "Cool, laid back, suave...broke!" And the orange dot would be a combination of the two: "He's gonna screw you over, but he'll be so good at it you won't care."

— Cathie Boruch

I hate that book *Men Are From Mars, Women Are From Venus* because men aren't from Mars, men are from women. Men come out of women, so if they're screwed up, it's all our fault; stop trying to blame it on other planets.

— Cathyrn Michon

If you lower your standards, there are men everywhere!

— Debbie Kasper

My mother says, "Date professional men. *Professional* men!" As opposed to what, amateurs? It's just a hobby with them, they're only men on weekends?

— Ellen Orchid

Men are like flowers. If you don't know how to handle a rose, you get stuck by a couple of pricks.

— Margot Black

Men. You give them an inch, they add it to their own.

— Barbara Scott

If there were no women in the world, men would be naked, driving trucks, living in dirt. Women came along and gave us a reason to comb our hair.

— Sinbad

Men are stupid and women are crazy. And the reason women are so crazy is because men are so stupid.

— George Carlin

Men are like pay phones. Some of them take your money. Most of them don't work, and when you find one that does, someone else is on it.

— Catherine Franco

Men and women are a lot alike in certain situations. Like when they're both on fire, they're exactly alike.

— Dave Attell

What do men want? Men want a mattress that cooks.

— Judy Tenuta

When I think of some of the men I've slept with—if they were women, I wouldn't have had lunch with them.

— Carol Siskind

I like my men the way I like my subways: hot, packed, and unloading every three minutes.

— Judy Tenuta

Men are hunters, women are gatherers. Men risk death to bring back meat. Women bring back useful things like fruit, water, and hunters.

— **Basil White**

I know what men want. Men want to be really, really close to someone who will leave them alone.

— **Elayne Boosler**

My mom always said, "Men are like linoleum floors. You lay them right, and you can walk on them for thirty years."

— **Brett Butler**

My perfect man is smart, funny, good-looking, a good dresser, sensitive, and he won't chase other women. So what I figured out is that my perfect man is gay.

— **Karen Haber**

It's difficult to resist charming men, they're like chocolate. You think you can have just one bite, and you end up eating the whole bar. It's a visual. A rich one.

— **Caryl Fuller**

The only perfect man is Mr. Ed. He's hung like a horse, and can hold a conversation.

— Traci Skene

A good man doesn't just happen. They have to be created by us women. A guy is a lump, like a dough-nut. So first, you gotta get rid of all the stuff his mom did to him. And then you gotta get rid of all that macho stuff they pick up from beer commercials. And then there's my personal favorite, the male ego.

— Roseanne Barr

I like lazy men because they make me feel like I'm getting stuff done.

— Rosie Tran

I figure the only time I really need a man is about once a month, when it's time to flip my mattress.

— Pamela Yager

Men do not like to admit to even momentary imper-fection. My husband forgot the code to turn off the alarm. When the police came, he wouldn't admit he'd forgotten the code. He turned himself in.

— Rita Rudner

Men and women belong to different species and communications between them is still in its infancy.

— Bill Cosby

It seems to me that men ask a lot of questions, but they're not willing to do the research. They're always asking, "What do women want? What do women want?" Why don't they try buying us a bunch of stuff and see what happens?

— **Livia Squires**

Men are delusional. Hugh Hefner lounges around in a bathrobe with three live-in girlfriends. You know guys are sitting at home watching the Playboy channel and thinking, "That could be me. *I've* got a bathrobe."

— **Denise Munro Robb**

Men don't settle down. Men surrender.

— **Chris Rock**

Guys, have you ever been quiet for a minute around your girl? What's the first thing women ask? "What are you thinking?" And guys always reply, "Nothing." Ladies, believe them! They can actually do that. Leave the man alone. If you keep bugging him, he's gonna be thinking, "Will you shut the fuck up? *That's* what I was thinking."

— **Wanda Sykes**

If you want your man to totally worship you like a love goddess, act like a Ferrari: make a lot of noise, and only start when he puts all of his money into you.

— **Judy Tenuta**

I like manly men. I like you to do man stuff. I ain't that type of woman to be like, "Ooh, he won't go to the mall with me." I don't need you at the mall, okay? I know my role. You make the money, *I* spend it.

— Tess

The quickest way to a man's heart is through his chest.

— Roseanne Barr

* MÉNAGE Á TROIS *

It seems like we hear more talk about the threesome in sex. And when I was single that was sincerely never a fantasy of mine. It was never like, "How could I wake up with two disappointed ladies tomorrow?"

— Bob Goldthwait

The closest I ever came to a *ménage à trois* was once I dated a schizophrenic.

— Rita Rudner

I was out dancing, and this couple hit on me. They wanted to swing! What can you say when you've been propositioned by a couple? I was thinking really fast, and said, "As a matter of fact, I'm already seeing a couple. And they'd be livid if I cheated on them."

— Kathy Griffin

I'm not an advocate of three-way sex. They're like that Lucy episode where Lucy and Ethel are trying to stuff all the chocolate into their mouths. I tried a five-way once, but I'm too needy. Afterwards I was like, "So are we all in a relationship now?"

— Margaret Cho

* MENSTRUATION *

I hate my period because it interrupts my life. Last month I couldn't have sex for a whole week. But it's better than the alternative: kids interrupt every day of the month.

— Johnnye Jones Gibson

* MIRRORS *

I have tried a little kinky stuff. A woman called me and said, "I have mirrors all over my bedroom. Bring a bottle." I brought Windex.

— *Rodney Dangerfield*

I heard that having a mirror over your bed was supposed to be romantic. A week later I caught somebody shoplifting in my apartment.

— *Elayne Boosler*

* MISTER RIGHT *

I married Mr. Right. Mr. *Always* Right.

— *Lotus Weinstock*

* MONEY *

I realized that I like to date men who make less money than I do. But surprisingly, it's equally as hard to get the homeless to commit.

— *Rosalie Bahmer*

An average guy makes a date with a girl. It costs him one hundred dollars, two hundred dollars. I make a date with a girl, it costs me nothing. I come up to her house. She wants to go out. I let her go! What's my business? I have to follow her around?

— Jackie Mason

I'm so broke I'm actually considering getting a second boyfriend.

— Christina Walkinshaw

It costs a lot of money to date. I took a girl out to dinner the other night. I said, "What'll you have?" She said, "I guess I'll have the steak and lobster." I said, "Guess again."

— Skip Stephenson

My mother always said, "Don't marry for money. Divorce for money."

— Wendy Liebman

* MONOGAMY *

I meet guys who have absolutely no concept of monogamy, they think it's a game by Milton Bradley.

— Cathy Ladman

Monogamy is really weird, like when you know their name and everything.

— Margaret Cho

Being married is like getting to have your favorite soft drink any time you want. But only your favorite soft drink. It's monogamous. You feel like a hot drink, you better heat up some Mr. Pibb.

— Jeff Cesario

Monogamous sex isn't boring. It's like a really great book that you don't want to end— and then it doesn't.

— Beth Lapides

If variety is the spice of life, marriage is the big can of leftover Spam.

— Johnny Carson

A study shows that monogamous couples live longer. And cheaters who don't get caught live longer than cheaters who do get caught.

— Jay Leno

That's why I'm afraid of marriage. You have to make love to the same person for, like, three hundred years. How do you keep it exciting? Hats?

— *Elayne Boosler*

It can take a man several marriages to understand the importance of monogamy.

— *Jason Love*

* MOTHERS *

When I was younger, I'd go out with men who lived with their mother. Now if I'm with a man who lives with his mother, her last name better be Streisand or Trump.

— *Sunda Croonquist*

My mother said to me, "Don't sleep with a man, until he buys you a house." Well, it worked for her, and I got a swing set out of the deal.

— *Judy Brown*

* MOVIES *

My boyfriend won't see anything he terms a "chick film." That's any film where the woman talks.

— *Maura Lake*

My wife and I have different tastes in movies: I like good ones, and she likes the bad ones.

— Jason Love

I've been in a few interracial relationships and I have a little tip for you. Never go see the movie *Amistad* on the first date.

— Kelli Dunham

I really detest movies like *Indecent Proposal* and *Pretty Woman* because they send the message to women that sleeping with a rich man is the ultimate goal, and really, that's such a small part of it.

— Laura Kightlinger

I've always tried to be as cool as the Bond girls, but they don't remind me of any women I know. Sleeping with him one second, forgetting him the next. Where is the Bond girl who says, "James, I know we discovered the antidote to a rare tropical virus that threatened to destroy the earth, but why didn't you call? And who's that Korean kick-boxer you're with? Did our trip in the submarine mean nothing?"

— Maura Lake

My sex life is sometimes like Murphy's Law, if something can go wrong, it will. Like one time during sex, my IUD started picking up radio stations. And what's worse is my boyfriend said, "Don't move. That's a really good song." All I can say is, if you've never seen a naked man play air guitar, count your blessings.

— *Maria Menozzi*

I think my neighbor broke up with his girlfriend last night because he played "Ain't No Sunshine When She's Gone" thirteen times in a row.

— *Wendy Wilkins*

The hardest thing about getting out of a relationship is listening to the radio. Because every song is about being in love, or being heartbroken. And I found that the only song I was comfortable with is that Peter, Paul and Mary song, "If I Had a Hammer."

— *Ellen DeGeneres*

If you break up you can't listen to the radio. "You're listening to the All-Love-Songs station, nothing but stick-your-head-in-the-oven and turn-up-the-gas love songs. And now for everybody who just broke up, here's a song you'll enjoy, 'You'll be Alone for the Rest of your Life' from the CD, *You'll Die in a Puddle of Your Own Urine in a Welfare Hospital.*"

— Richard Jeni

They say violent music lyrics make men mistreat women. I think if a man is going to treat you bad, he's going to treat you bad, he doesn't need theme music.

— Leighann Lord

* NEIGHBORS *

You know those annoying neighbors who keep you up in the middle of the night, banging that bed, hitting the wall, and screaming with pleasure? Well that's me! Be happy for me; I'm building a relationship.

— Chantel Rae

* OBSESSIONS *

Irrational crushes, infatuations, or obsessions. Whatever you want to label it, it's important to reach out to others.

— Janeane Garofalo

* OLDER MEN *

I married an older man. Foreplay took a little longer, but at least his hand shook.

— Jenny Jones

The last guy I dated was older than I am, and he loved to take me dancing. But do you know how difficult it is to dance with a guy who has a walker?

— Stacey Prussman

The old saying was, "Marry an older man because they're mature." The saying now is, "Marry a young man because men don't mature."

— Rita Rudner

There ain't nothing an old man can do but bring me a message from a young one.

— Moms Mabley

* ORGASMS *

In a lifetime the average person spends four hours out of 569,500 hours experiencing orgasm. And 62% of that is self-inflicted.

— Lily Tomlin

Everyone has a different way to reach orgasm. For me everything has to be in harmony, my yin has got to be totally balanced with my checkbook.

— Simone Alexander

My boyfriend's always saying, "I can never tell if you've had an orgasm. I can never tell." I said, "Well, turn off the TV and get in here."

— Livia Squires

I overheard these two young guys talking about women and sex. One guy says, "It's so much easier for women to have an orgasm on top." And the other guy argued, "No, it's easier for women to have an orgasm when she's on the bottom." Finally, I turned to them and said, "Guys, actually it's much easier when we're alone."

— Cory Kahaney

Women might be able to fake orgasms. But men can fake whole relationships.

— Jimmy Shubert

Guys wonder why we fake it. It's called "time management." I don't need to be up all night working on something that's not going to happen, you're just cutting into my sleep time. He's working hard at making something happen, you already know it ain't gonna happen, and you glance at the clock, "Shoot, it's 1:30 in the morning and I got to get up at six. To hell with this—*Oh yes! Oh yes, baby!*"

— *Wanda Sykes*

I once had a girlfriend who was so guilt-ridden about being a lesbian that the only way she could have an orgasm was if we pretended to be shipwrecked, adrift at sea, far from civilization, never to return. So in order to make this whole thing realistic, I had to buy an inflatable raft, a foot pump, and a bailing bucket. Then I had another girlfriend who liked sex best under time pressure, when she had to rush. So we used to pretend that she was an air traffic controller who had ten seconds to come before two jumbo jets would collide in midair. That was exciting, the best nine and a half seconds of my life.

— *Sara Cytron*

* ORGIES *

I could never be comfortable at an orgy. I'd always think there would be someone making rabbit ears behind my back.

— *Diane Nichols*

* PARENTS *

I read that in every generation the kids are supposed to surpass the parents. I'm not any taller, or earning more money, but I do have a much worse marriage, so I'm ahead that way.

— *Janet Rosen*

I recently met my girlfriend's parents. Before I was afraid they wouldn't like me, now I know they don't.

— *Jayson Cross*

* PERFUME *

Why are women wearing perfume that smells like flowers when men don't like flowers? I've been wearing a great scent, it's called New Car Interior.

— *Rita Rudner*

✳ PERSONAL ADS ✳

Personal ads are written in a creepy code. "Likes long walks on the beach" and "quiet evenings at home," mean he wants to have sex, without having to spend money on you first. Anyone who describes himself as a "teddy bear" is morbidly obese. And don't go out with man looking for someone who "likes to try new things," unless you want to end up naked and handcuffed to a water pipe.

— Meg Maly

I'm embarrassed to admit it, but I've tried online dating. I haven't met anyone in person yet because the guys always stop writing before we can set up a date. I don't know what it is. Perhaps that handsome athletic thirty-two-year-old doctor was lying about his age, got grounded, and lost his internet privileges. Or maybe it was something I said, "I'd love to meet for coffee. Thursdays are best for me. That's when my neighbor picks up my four kids from my three previous marriages."

— Lori Giarnella

Someone emailed me from a personals Web site, "I like hiking, biking, camping and skiing." I wrote back, "While you're hiking, biking, camping and skiing, I'll be eating, drinking, sleeping and smoking. We're soul mates!"

— Michele Balan

My cousin Larry meets a lot of women now that he has changed his email address. He had a lot of trouble getting action with his old one, which was "36-year-old-living-with-my-mama@home.com."

— Robert Murray

A truly honest personal ad would say, "I want to date myself, only with more money."

— Maureen Brownsey

I saw a personal ad that looked interesting. It said she loved long walks, running on the beach, going to parks. As it turns out, she was a German shepherd.

— David Corrado

Saw this personal ad in the paper, "Democratic man would like to meet young woman Republican. Object: Third party."

— Henny Youngman

My sister married a great guy she met through an online dating service. I don't like to pry, but last week I finally got the nerve to ask her which one. She said she tried several, but eBay was the best.

— Katherine Poehlmann

You have to be careful with personal ads. I met a girl who described herself as statuesque. Turns out, she was covered in a thin green film and pigeons liked to sit on her.

— Craig Sharf

* PHONE SEX *

I have so much phone sex that if I had a child it would be born with a dial tone.

— Paulara R. Hawkins

Phone sex on cell phones is so frustrating. Every time it starts getting good, the phone starts cutting out. I'm like, "Honey, I'm losing you. Can you feel me now? Can you feel me now?"

— Dava Krause

What's embarrassing about phone sex is that the neighbors can hear me having sex, but they don't see anyone enter or leave my apartment.

— Sue Kolinsky

There are 25,000 sex phone lines for men in the U.S. but only three for women. Apparently, when we want somebody to talk dirty and nasty to us we just go to work.

— Felicia Michaels

I'm not embarrassed about having called one of those phone-sex lines. I dialed 976-HERS, just for the gals. My ex-lover answered. It was just like old times: she came, we fought about the cats, and I paid for sex.

— Karen Ripley

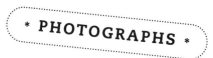
My boyfriend broke up with me last year for about two months. So I tore up all the photos I had with him in the picture. We got back together, and now he wants people to take pictures of us all the time. That's fine, but I leave just a little bit of space between us now in the picture. Just in case something happens and I look really good in that one.

— Mary Gallagher

I'm so bad at relationships, I haven't made a holiday twice with the same person. I have a box full of pictures of *Our First Christmas Together*.

— Michele Balan

In 1947 the Polaroid camera was invented. The next day the inventor assured his girlfriend, "I won't show these to anybody."

— Conan O'Brien

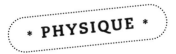

* PHYSIQUE *

Feeling shitty about your physique is an important state of mind, for it leads one into a series of diverse, unfulfilling relationships. As opposed to just one monogamous journey into the banal.

— Janeane Garofalo

* PICKUPS *

I have really good luck at picking up men in bars. It's amazing, I can pick up two to three guys at a time, all thanks to my weight-lifting coach and steroids.

— Andrea Henry

I'm standing on line at the bakery, and this really cute guy asked for my number. So I had to get another one.

— Wendy Liebman

For some women, picking up guys is just a sport. They don't intend to sleep with anyone; they just want to know that they could. Catch and release, catch and release.

— Jason Love

I met a guy in line at the post office. He said. "With a face like yours I feel like I can tell you anything." And he did. "I lost my last four jobs, they fired me, and my car got repossessed." So, I gave him my phone number. He called and said, "I'm calling from the Laundromat, my phone has been shut off, and I'm running out of change, but I'd like to take you out. For a walk." I replied, "Oh, no, I don't do things like *that* on a first date."

— Debbie Sue Goodman

* PLANS *

All plans between men are tentative, if one man should have an opportunity to pursue a woman. It doesn't matter how important the arrangements are: when they scrub a space shuttle launch, it's because an astronaut met someone on his way to the launch pad. They hold the countdown; he's leaning against the rocket talking to her, "What do you say we get together for some Tang?"

— Jerry Seinfeld

* PORNOGRAPHY *

My husband says I don't understand pornography because I'm always fast-forwarding to the story.

— Alicia Brandt

Women don't like porno, we like erotica. Rent us sexy films with love and romance, get a bottle of the good stuff—Boone's Farm Strawberry Hill—and they'll be nothing left to you but a rumor and a baseball cap.

— Monique Marvez

* PREMATURE EJACULATION *

My psychologist told me that a lot of men suffer from premature ejaculation. That's not true: women suffer.

— Robert Schimmel

* PRENUPTIAL AGREEMENTS *

My husband and I didn't sign a prenuptial agreement. We signed a mutual suicide pact.

— Roseanne Barr

* PROMISCUITY *

My sister was so promiscuous she broke her ankle in the glove compartment of a car.

— Phyllis Diller

My sister is a slut. She has this little ritual. She does this every morning. She gets up. She checks the mail so she can find the address, calls a cab, and gets herself the hell home.

— **Bonnie McFarlane**

* REAL ESTATE *

I was tagging along house hunting with married friends when they got into a heated discussion about whether they wanted to buy a three or four bedroom house. The husband screams at the wife, "How many *#@*^# kids do you want, anyhow?" She said, "I guess that depends on who the father is going to be."

— **Mary Pfeiffer**

* REBOUND *

I realize I'm the biggest superhero of them all: Rebound Girl. I'm the girl who gets the guy's apartment ready for his next girlfriend. Just like Mother Teresa had a calling to work with the lepers, it's my calling to work with...well, lepers. I don't know how these guys find out about me, it's as though a business card is passed around that says, "Got dumped? Call Eileen. Nice girl. Low maintenance. Will work for video rental and a pizza."

— Eileen Budd

* RECYCLING *

I have a friend who's so into recycling she'll only marry a man who's been married before.

— Rita Rudner

* RELATIONSHIPS *

There are two stages to the beginning of a relationship. Stage one is the fun stage, stage two sucks. Stage one is when you get to know the other person. Stage two is when you know them.

— Sue Schwartz

I'm not shooting for a successful relationship at this point. I am just looking for something that will prevent me from throwing myself in front of a bus. I'm keeping my expectations very, very low. Basically I'm looking for a mammal.

— Janeane Garofalo

I deserve someone who likes me for who I am pretending to be.

— Arj Barker

Honesty is the key to a relationship. If you can fake that, you're in.

— Richard Jeni

At the beginning of a relationship, wouldn't it save so much time if you could just ask the guy, "Hey, are you an asshole?" And the guy, could say, "Yeah." Which would be okay with me, because I go out with assholes. Exclusively.

— Karen Haber

The thing that makes me really annoying in relationships, makes me really good as a telemarketer.

— Denise Munro Robb

If you want to have a solid relationship someday, for the next year, date horrible women. You'll learn what to look out for. A bitch in time saves nine.

— Troy Conrad

I'm involved in a relationship because I figured, "Hey, what could be worse than dating?"

— **Garry Shandling**

Relationships don't last anymore. When I meet a guy, the first question I ask myself is: "Is this the man I want my children to spend their weekends with?"

— **Rita Rudner**

Men and women just look at life completely different. Women are playing chess, we plan relationships ten moves ahead. Meanwhile, the guy is playing checkers, thinking just one move ahead, "Jump me!"

— **Margot Black**

Never assume that the guy understands that you and he have a relationship.

— **Dave Barry**

I had a long-distance relationship, but it was too much work. So I decided to move to the city where he was. But then he changed his name—again—and notified the local authorities.

— **Andrea Henry**

If you are married or living with someone, then there is one thing that gets said day and night that drives both of you absolutely crazy. But one or both of you always say it. It is "What?" The word, the phrase, the implication, the irritation. "What?" "You're deaf?" you mumble. "What?" "I don't mumble, stupid." "I heard that." "*That* you heard."

— Elayne Boosler

The difference between being in a relationship and being in prison is that in prison they let you play softball on the weekends.

— Bobby Kelton

Couples always end up calling each other by cute pet names. Honey, Sweetie, Good-for-nothing, cheating loser. Maybe that's just me.

— Rosie Tran

I didn't have sex for a long time. I have a boyfriend now, and I still don't have sex, because we live together. Now that the milk is free, we've both become lactose-intolerant.

— Margaret Cho

Long distance relationships are hard. Especially when you both only have cell phones. It's like I don't become a girlfriend until nine P.M.

— Dava Krause

I just moved in with my boyfriend after having a two-year long-distance relationship. It's nice to do things together for a change. It's nice to go to the movies, have dinner together. Frankly, it's nice to have sex without having MCI involved.

— Sue Kolinsky

There are stages to relationships. Number one, intimate disclosure: when you want to get to know each other and you confess all your weird college drug experiences. Stage two is happy coasting, it's all going so smoothly and it's always going to be like this. Number three: shut-the-fuck-up. Four: embittered silence. Like when you see old couples in the restaurant not talking, just playing chess with the salt and pepper shakers. And if you're lucky, the final stage: memory loss. You go back to talking about your drugs, only this time they're not the fun ones, they're prescription.

— Janet Rosen

Relationships should come with coupons and an expiration date: "My love for you is good until
_____."

— Michele Balan

I can't get a relationship to last longer than it takes to burn their CDs.

— **Margaret Smith**

You always know when the relationship is over. Little things start grating on your nerves, "Would you please stop that! That breathing in and out, it's so repetitious!"

— **Ellen DeGeneres**

Relationships are hard. It's like a full-time job, and we should treat it like one. If your boyfriend or girlfriend wants to leave you, they should give you two weeks' notice. There should be severance pay, and before they leave you, they have to find you a temp.

— **Bob Ettinger**

I can't seem to make a relationship work. I'd give up trying if it weren't for all the cool parting gifts. You know, the stuff a guy leaves at your place he's not getting back. That's how I got half my CD collection, and all my porn.

— **Joanna Briley**

I love to shop after a bad relationship. I buy a new outfit and it makes me feel better. It just does. Sometimes if I see a really great outfit, I'll break up with someone on purpose.

— **Rita Rudner**

I just got out of a five-year relationship, with four different people.

— Michele Balan

When I'm not in a relationship, I shave one leg. So when I sleep, it feels like I'm with a woman.

— Garry Shandling

Some women go from one relationship to the next. Not me. It takes me forever to find a guy worse than the one I was just with.

— LeMaire

I'm not in a relationship now, but I have a stalker. Which is kind of nice, because at least he calls. And I never have to make plans with him, because he's always there for me.

— Pamela Yager

* RELIGION *

I'm Catholic, and my mother said we were born to suffer. So I married an attorney.

— Maura Lake

My husband thought reincarnation means you come back as a carnation.

— Phyllis Diller

I thought about being a nun for a while, and believed I'd make a god-darned good nun. Then I had sex and thought, "Well, fuck *that*."

— Diane Ford

Went out with a Jehovah's Witness once. It was the longest date of my life: we had to make like twenty stops before dinner.

— Debbie Kasper

* REMARRIAGE *

My wife and I got remarried. Our divorce didn't work out.

— Henny Youngman

I don't understand couples who break up and get back together, especially couples who divorce and remarry. That's like pouring milk on a bowl of cereal, tasting it and saying, "This milk is sour. Well, I'll put it back in the refrigerator, maybe it will be okay tomorrow."

— Larry Miller

Remarrying a husband you've divorced is like having your appendix put back in.

— Phyllis Diller

This is my second marriage and I've learned, grown. If we have a fight, before we go to bed I always say three little words, "I love you." If that doesn't work I say two little words: "Community property."

— Joanne Astrow

I feel my second marriage has finally prepared me for my first.

— Michael Feldman

My mom is on her eighth husband. Federal legislation to keep gay people from getting hitched was called the "Defense of Marriage Act," but if they really want to defend marriage they'd pass a law that prohibits my mother from coming within 100 yards of a Las Vegas wedding chapel.

— Kelli Dunham

I just got married. It's my husband's second marriage. If you think it's hard to get a guy who's never been married to commit, try to get a guy to go back and do it all over again. It's like talking a vet back into Vietnam.

— Cory Kahaney

My dad was married six times and yet he's always trying to teach me stuff about women. He says, "You know my first wife, Barbara — " "Diane, Dad." "Diane, right. She would ..."

— Rob Twohy

My mom's been married seven times to seven different drunks. Talk about faith in the institution of marriage! What's her thought process? "Well, my last six marriages to alcoholics led to financial ruin, emotional chaos, and the disintegration of my immediate family. But this time it's going to be different: I've finally chosen the right alcoholic!"

— Kelli Dunham

I'd like to get married again. I miss the daily experience of making someone miserable.

— JeanAnn O'Brien

I'm on my second marriage. You know when you let one guy get away, you're gonna have to build a taller fence and put better food out.

— Brett Butler

I'm going to marry again because I'm more mature now, and I need some kitchen stuff.

— Wendy Liebman

* RESPECT *

I met a guy the other night, I went home with him, I was going to have sex with him that night, but at the last minute I thought better of it. But I wound up staying over anyway. The next morning I changed my mind and had sex with him in the morning, which was nice and all, but then I spent the whole day wondering if he would respect me in the evening.

— Lynn Harris

Instead of asking a guy if he'll respect you in the morning, you should ask, "Do you have a job in the morning?"

— Bonnie Cheeseman

* RESTAURANTS *

Have you ever been in a restaurant and a couple in the next booth is being overly affectionate? They're necking and groping, and you're trying to eat your eggs. I always want to go up to them and say, "Excuse me, mind if I join you?" What are these people thinking? Do they wake up in the morning and ask each other, "Want to have sex, honey?" "No, let's wait until we get to Denny's."

— Bobby Kelton

If I ever got money, I would open a restaurant for single people. And I'd make 'em feel comfortable, too. Name it Just One. You walk in, nice long row of sinks. No tables and chairs. Everyone eats standing over the sink. All the food comes in the package, so you can read the back while you're eating.

— Elayne Boosler

When going to a restaurant, "party of one" is rarely cause for celebration.

— Ellen DeGeneres

My husband has never picked up a check in his life. People think he has an impediment in his reach.

— Phyllis Diller

If you're a guy and you ask for the doggie bag on a date, you might as well have them wrap up your genitals, too. You're not going to be needing those for awhile, either.

— Jerry Seinfeld

I once dated a waitress. In the middle of sex she'd say, "How is everything? Is everything okay over here?"

— David Corrado

* ROLE PLAY *

My wife asked me if we could trade gender roles for a week, so she could sit around all the time and watch TV. I agreed, and then immediately started nagging her about how she watches too much TV.

— Jeff Scott

My husband and I were role playing the other night and I started to cry, when I realized that he'd cleaned the apartment.

— Alex House

I wanted my last girlfriend to get into role-playing in bed. But she would always say, "Just put the dice away."

— Myq Kaplan

* ROMANCE *

Walking in the rain is not romantic—it's called "getting the flu."

— Mike Lemme

Most women say they want romance. I'm willing to settle for a clean apartment and some Carl's Jr.

— Rosie Tran

Fifty percent of the American population spends less than ten dollars a month on romance. You know what we call these people? Men.

— Jay Leno

My mother always said that a rose is the perfect symbol of romance. It dies after a few days, its pretty petals fall off, and all you're left with is the ugly prickly thing.

— Maureen Murphy

* SAFE SEX *

Remember when safe sex meant your parents had gone away for the weekend?

— Rhonda Hansome

Everybody should practice safe sex. Because nobody wants to be doing it and put an eye out.

— Emmy Gay

Safe sex is very important. That's why I'm never doing it on plywood scaffolding again.

— Jenny Jones

I practice safe sex. I use an airbag. It's a little startling at first when it flies out. Then the woman realizes it's safer than being thrown clear.

— Garry Shandling

Nothing I learned in school prepared me for life on any level. My first book should have read, "See Dick balance his checkbook. See Jane leave an unhealthy relationship. Run Jane run!"

— **Kate Mason**

In high school my sister went out with the captain of the chess team. My parents loved him. They figured that any guy who took hours to make a move was OK with them.

— **Brian Kiley**

I remember my prom, the limo, the dancing until dawn. It would have been even better if I'd had a date.

— **David Letterman**

A study shows the average high school prom-goer spends $1,000. Or $1,009, if you count the pregnancy test.

— **Jay Leno**

* SELF-ANALYSIS *

I won't get into this whole self-analysis thing, I just won't. And I don't have to, because my boyfriend will do it for me.

— Laura Kightlinger

* SELF-DESTRUCTION *

I'm not a very self-destructive person, but mostly because I'm too lazy. I prefer to be in a relationship and let someone else do the work.

— Margot Black

* SELF-ESTEEM *

This guy dumped me because he said I have a low self-esteem. I said, "No kidding, I slept with you, didn't I? "

— Tracey MacDonald

I'm currently dating a girl with no self-esteem. Which is good, because if she had any, she'd leave me.

— Devin Dugan

I have low self-esteem. When we were in bed together, I would fantasize that *I* was someone else.

— Richard Lewis

* SELF-INVOLVEMENT *

He was the most self-involved guy I ever met in my life. He had a coffee mug on his table that said, "I'm the Greatest." He had a plaque on the wall that said, "I'm Number One." And on his bedspread it said, "The Best." In the middle of making love he said, "Move over, you're getting in my way."

— Karen Haber

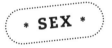

* SEX *

I told my girlfriend that Dr. Ruth compared men to a sexual microwave: they start fast and finish fast. And women are more like crock-pots: they take a long time to heat up, but can cook for hours. My girlfriend said, "Yeah, and you're like an old toaster that heats for ten seconds before it pops up."

— Joe Ditzel

How many women like to have sex in the morning? Now how many like to be awake when it happens?

— Marsha Warfield

Dr. Ruth says women should tell our lovers how to make love to us. My boyfriend goes nuts if I tell him how to drive.

— Pam Stone

It's too much trouble to get laid. Because you have to go out with a guy, and go to dinner with him, and listen to him talk about his opinions, and I don't have that kind of time.

— Kathy Griffin

Each person has their own sexual timetable of what should happen when. We need some sort of rule-book: standard dating procedure. "We've been out three times. According to Article 7, Section 5, there's got to be some physical contact. Otherwise, I will report you to the board, and they can put out a warrant for an embrace."

— Jerry Seinfeld

It's hard to date after divorce. And my therapist isn't making it easier: he said that you're supposed to wait four to six months before you have sex with a guy you're dating. I was stunned. How many relationships even last that long?

— Caryl Fuller

Once the sexual revolution took hold, people really didn't have to buy the cow to get the milk. And girls today are like the dairy barn. So guys don't feel the necessity to get married. And the girls don't either.

— Joy Behar

I'm afraid to give instructions in bed because I'm afraid I'll get carried away. "Okay, pull my hair, and touch me right there. No, to the left. Now go outside and move my car so I won't get a ticket. Yeah, that's it."

— Laura Kightlinger

Making love to a woman is like buying real estate: location, location, location.

— Carol Leifer

It's so long since I've had sex, I've forgotten who ties up whom.

— Joan Rivers

There are more important things than sex. I always thought that music was more important than sex. Then I noticed that if I don't hear a concert for a year and a half, it don't bother me.

— Jackie Mason

For guys sex is like going to a restaurant. No matter what they order off that menu, they walk out saying, "Damn, that was good!" For women it don't work like that. We go to the restaurant, sometimes it's good, sometimes we got to send it back. You have those hit and misses, you might want to skip a few meals. Or you might go, "I think I'm going to cook for myself today."

— Wanda Sykes

My favorite sexual position is rich man on top, me on the bottom, looking up at my new five-carat diamond ring saying, "Yes, Yes, Yes, you're so big!"

— Elaine Pelino

Guys always ask me how many men I've been with. Like I remember.

— Chantel Rae

A guy once asked me to talk to him in bed. So I said, "Is it in yet?"

— Janet Rosen

My last boyfriend liked to talk a lot during sex. He said it was because it turned him on, but I think he had ulterior motives because he always said the same thing, "Wake up, wake up, wake up!"

— Christine O'Rourke

Women are really not that exacting. They only desire one thing in bed. Take off your socks. And by the way — they're not going to invite their best girl-friend over for a three-some, so you can stop asking.

— **Dennis Miller**

I asked my wife to try anal sex. She said, "Sure. You first."

— **Robert Schimmel**

I'm not good in bed. Hell, I'm not even good on the couch.

— **Drew Carey**

I never believed in casual sex. I have always tried as hard as I could.

— **Garry Shandling**

The basic conflict between men and women sexually, is that men are like firemen. To us, sex is an emergency, and no matter what we're doing we can be ready in two minutes. Women are like fire. They're very exciting, but the conditions have to be exactly right for it to occur.

— **Jerry Seinfeld**

I'm in kind of a sexual dry spell. For the past few years, I've only had sex in the months that end in "arch."

— Doug Benson

Sex after children slows down. Every three months now we have sex. Every time I have sex, the next day I pay my quarterly taxes. Unless it's oral sex— then I renew my driver's license.

— Ray Romano

I asked my girlfriend who she fantasized about while we were having sex, and she said, "I don't really have time."

— Owen O'Neill

My wife insists on turning off the lights when we make love. That doesn't bother me. It's the hiding that seems so cruel.

— Jonathan Katz

There is a video out now on how to please men. Here's tip number one: just show up!

— Jay Leno

You know your sex life has dwindled when you get muscle soreness the next day after making love, like you just decided to take up running.

— Laura Hayden

Women need a reason to have sex. Men just need a place.

— Billy Crystal

Men reach their sexual peak at eighteen. Women reach their sexual peak at thirty-five. Do you get the feeling God is into practical jokes? We're reaching our sexual peak right around the same time they're discovering they have a favorite chair.

— Rita Rudner

I've been thinking about when you're old, or even when you're not so old, when it's the last time in your life that you have sex, do you know it's the last time? Or do you only look back later and go, "Oh no, *that* was it? I wish I'd made more special: lit a scented candle, clean sheets, not faked it, not done it with *you.*"

— Janet Rosen

Men perform oral sex like they drive. When they get lost they refuse to ask for directions.

— Catherine Franco

Ladies, sexually, if your man won't do it, his best friend will.

— Lewis Ramey

I asked my wife, "On a scale of one to ten, how do you rate me as a lover?" She said, "You know I'm no good at fractions."

— Rodney Dangerfield

I told my girlfriend that unless she expressed her feelings and told me what she liked, I wouldn't be able to please her. So she said, "Get off me."

— Garry Shandling

I got a weird sexual education. Most parents teach the birds and the bees. Mine showed me horror movies, where all the teenage characters having sex get killed, thinking it would discourage me. It didn't work. I still have sex, except now I say weird things while making out. Like, "What was that? Did you hear a noise?" and "The phone line has been cut. Where's Marsha?" And at the climactic moment, I always scream out, "You wait here, I'll go get help!"

— Chantel Rae

* SHOPPING *

My husband and I went to buy a lamp. We couldn't find one that we both liked, so we had to compromise and buy one that we both hated.

— Janet Rosen

* SINGLE *

I don't think of myself as single. I'm romantically challenged.

— Stephanie Piro

It bothers me that the world revolves around married people with children, so I've come up with a politically-correct term for Single with No Kids: Happy.

— Danielle Broussard

I'm single, but friends tell me it's because I'm a "quality" girl and quality people take longer to meet each other. But to me, "quality" sounds like a moth-eaten dress in a vintage store. I want to be cheap and in demand, like the stuff that flies off the rack at the Gap.

— Cathie Boruch

I'm single by choice. Not my choice.

— **Orny Adams**

When you're first single, you're so optimistic. At the beginning, you're like, "I want to meet a guy who's really smart, really sweet, really good-looking, has a really great career. Six months later, you're like, "Lord, any mammal with a day job."

— **Carol Leifer**

I'm not good at being alone. Especially at the end of the day when my finances are a mess, my car is falling apart, I can't find my shoe. That's when I need a big strong guy to hold me close so I can look deep into his eyes, and blame him.

— **Simone Alexander**

I just want a man who's both politically, and anatomically, correct.

— **Ellen Orchid**

I hate singles events. This one guy walks up to me wearing a nametag with "P.A." on it, and I think, "Hey, at last, an honest man who admits he's passive-aggressive." But, no, it turns out he's advertising that he's poly-amorous: he wants to have several lovers in the same room at the same time. I'm a single mom who's dating, and all I could think was, "What a scheduling nightmare!"

— **Caryl Fuller**

The thing I hate about living alone is living alone. I have way too many frivolous conversations with the 411 operator.

— Sue Bova

I got married to complicate my thought process. When you're single, your brain is single-minded. Single guys think three things: "I'd like to go out with her," "I'd like to buy one of those," and "I hope those guys win."

— Jerry Seinfeld

You know you've been single too long when you call the Jehovah's Witnesses to ask them why they haven't been around lately.

— Debbie Kasper

I'm forty and single. Don't you think it's a generalization that you should be married at forty? That's like looking at somebody who's seventy and saying, "Hey, when are you gonna break your hip? All your friends are breaking their hips—what are you waiting for?"

— Sue Kolinsky

I joined a singles group in my neighborhood. The president called me up and asked, "I want to find out what kind of activities you like to plan." I said, "Well, weddings."

— Lynn Harris

Every single one of my friends from high school has long since tied the knot. And I'm getting older, I guess I should think about hanging myself, too.

— Laura Kightlinger

* SLEEPING *

A friend of mine is handicapped and in a wheelchair, but in his dreams he runs and jumps and plays. Which makes sense, because in my dreams I'm single and have no children.

— Jason Love

In bed my wife sprawls out all over the mattress. I said, "I'm tired of only having two inches in this bed." She said "Now you know how I feel."

— Peter Sasso

My wife likes to spoon in bed...yeah, I know. But I do what I've got to do. The other night we spooned in bed for thirty minutes, then I forked her brains out.

— Jason Love

* SMELL *

Men and women both care about smell, but women go to the trouble to smell good. Men are like, "Does this stink too bad to wear one more time? Maybe I should iron it."

— Jeff Foxworthy

* STOOD UP *

My sister's yearlong jerk boyfriend blew her off for a date, and she freaked out. I'm like "Sara, relax, you don't know what happened. Think positive: maybe he died."

— Laurie McDermott

* STRIPPERS *

One of my friends was getting married, and they tell me I have to chip in for a male stripper. Are you out of your damn mind? I ain't paying for no naked-ass man. Women don't have to pay to see that. We spend most of our time trying *not* to see that.

— Wanda Sykes

My friends hired a male stripper for my birthday present. This guy starts throwing his clothes off, and asks me, "What are you thinking, baby?" I'm thinking I've been married too long, because I said, "You're going to pick up after yourself, aren't you?

— Mary Pfeiffer

* SWIMMING *

Don't go skinny-dipping with Greenpeace members; they don't believe in offshore drilling.

— Daniel Liebert

* TATTOOS *

Couples who get tattooed are the most optimistic people in the world about relationships. I don't want a former lover's name in my phone book, much less his picture on my ass.

— Carol Siskind

A friend of mine had his girlfriend's name tattooed on his arm. Now, I can see marrying a girl and having a few kids. But a tattoo...It's so permanent.

— Drake Sather

* TEENAGE *

I was too young when I got married: nineteen. They ought to lock up nineteen year-old girls in closets until those hormones stop playing ping-pong with their brains. Because I was walking stupidly looking for a place to land.

— Diane Ford

* TELEPHONES *

I borrowed my brother's cell phone, because mine was broken—after my girlfriend discovered how many other women's telephone numbers came up in the memory.

— Matze Knop

* TELEPHONE CALLS *

I don't want to brag, but back in the day I used to get a lot of calls from guys. There was a time when I had something that they didn't have and they really, really wanted it. They'd beg me for it. They had to have it that night. Answers to the homework.

— Lori Giarnella

I have bad luck with women. A woman I was dating told me on the phone, "I have to go, there's a tele-marketer on the other line."

— Zach Galifiankis

Men will say, "I'll call you. I'll call you." When they say they're going to call, they don't, and when they say they're not going to come, they do.

— Carol Henry

Guys keep calling, and calling, and they won't stop. So I wondered, what's the one thing a girl can do to make guys stop calling? Oh yeah, sleep with them.

— Chantel Rae

I don't like the idea that people can call you in your car. I think there's news you shouldn't get at sixty miles per hour. "Pregnant? Whoaah!"

— Tom Parks

They say they're going to call you at about seven o'clock. It's seven and they haven't called. So you say, okay, I'll fix myself a drink. So you have a drink, then you have another, then you have another, and you have another. Now you're drunk. It's five after seven and they still haven't called.

— Ellen DeGeneres

* TELEPHONE NUMBERS *

When women don't want to give out their phone number, they make up a number. This one girl said to me, "My telephone number? 4,5,6 - 7,8,9,10." "Is that by any chance in the 1,2,3 area code?"

— Ron Richards

Men, if you've ever been given a fake phone number, it means you scare women. Basically, it says, "I'd reject you to your face, but I'm afraid that my head would wind up in the garbage and my body in the bay. So here's a phony phone number. Hopefully, you won't figure that out until I've made my escape."

— Lori Chapman

When women don't wanna give out their phone number, they ask the guy for his number instead, "No, I'll call you." Then they take out a piece of chalk, "What is it?"

— Ron Richards

Is there anyone left who thinks they're going to hear good news when asked by their lover to go on the *Jerry Springer* Show?

— JeanAnn O'Brien

My wife loves those reality shows on The Learning Channel: *Dating Story, Wedding Story, Baby Story.* They follow different couples through all those major events, but they're always just a little too perfect for me. Just once, I'd like to see a more realistic version. Instead of *Dating Story*, the *We Got Drunk and Hooked Up Story*, followed by the sequel, *"Uh Oh, Got Knocked Up, We're Having a Baby Story."*

— Tony Deyo

I don't like to channel surf. You guys like it don't you? You like to change the channel. We like to change you.

— Wendy Liebman

Whenever you want to get your man's attention, throw the word "remote" in the conversation. "Honey, *(blank stare)* there's a remote *(full attention)* possibility that my family will be over for dinner."

— Mary Pfeiffer

Women, please realize that men also need quality time with the television.

— Jason Love

* TOOTHBRUSHES *

My girlfriend used my toothbrush, so I bought two more: a dark blue toothbrush and a pink one. Of course, my girlfriend took the dark blue one, leaving me to buy a third toothbrush.

— Tim Homayoon

* TRANSSEXUALS *

I met this transsexual at my gym and he was telling me about how he had a sex change to become a woman, and now he's started to date other women. I said, "Look, fellow/ma'am, I think you are making this a little bit harder than it has to be."

— Shashi Bhatia

* TRAUMAS *

I'm suffering from post-post-traumatic syndrome, and I'm going to keep talking about it until some cute guy holds me.

— Kathy Griffin

* TRAVEL *

I've always wanted to date a man who travels. Dreams do come true; I'm now seeing a bus driver.

— Julie Kidd

* UNDRESSING *

According to a new survey, women say they feel more comfortable undressing in front of men than they do undressing in front of other women. They say that women are too judgmental, where, of course, men are just grateful.

— *Jay Leno*

* UNIFORMS *

They say women love a man in uniform. It's true. The uniform sends a clear message: he has a job.

— *Mimi Gonzalez*

* VACATIONS *

My girlfriend got upset during our vacation: "This beach is polluted. That poor seagull is covered in oil." And I said, "Bullshit, this is a nude beach. That's a kinky gull in a latex suit."

— *Matze Knop*

* VIAGRA *

My last boyfriend took Viagra and it kept him aroused for four hours. But after the sex, what do you do for the remaining three hours and fifty-seven minutes. Do they make a drug for that?

— Stacey Prussman

Viagra is the work of the devil. Now we girls can look forward to having sex with really old guys for a really long time.

— Le Maire

* VIDEO *

Friends sent me a videotape of their wedding. I accidentally fast-forwarded right to the divorce.

— Denise Munro Robb

It was the thiry-fifth anniversary of the camcorder. It was also the thiry-fifth anniversary of the saying, "Come on baby, I swear nobody will see this but us."

— Jennifer Vally

* VIRGINITY *

The most precious gift you can give to a man is your virginity. I ought to know, I've given it to at least a dozen men.

— Livia Squires

I don't think a woman should be a virgin before marriage. She should have had at least one other disappointing experience.

— Maureen Murphy

* WEDDING GIFTS *

What if we wrote what we were really thinking on wedding gift thank you notes? "Thank you so much for the St. Patrick's Day pitcher and glassware set. Thank you especially for the box that it came in because that made throwing out the entire set all at once much easier."

— Jeff Scott

My wedding was great. Everyone said we should register at a department store, but we wanted cash so we registered at Bank of America.

— Denise Munro Robb

You know what the best part of getting married is? Opening the envelopes. That way you get to see how cheap your relatives really are.

— Joey Callahan

* WEDDING RINGS *

I like a man who wears a wedding ring. Because without it, they're like a shark without a fin. You pretty much got to know they're out there.

— Brett Butler

* WEDDINGS *

Once you're in a relationship, everybody wants to know, "When's the wedding, when's the wedding?" I'm on to them, they're only asking because they want a party. Why should my life be ruined just because you want to get smashed and eat cake? There's a bakery and a liquor store in every town. You can become a fat alcoholic on your own, leave me out of it.

— Lee Arleth

Weddings are expensive. My father married off both my sisters. He said it was like buying a brand-new Mercedes, driving it to the hall, and leaving it there.

— Modi

Some men ask, "What's the point of a wedding?" But if you're going to commit to one woman for the rest of your life, you might as well get a George Foreman Grill.

— Steve Boyer

If the wedding invitations were left up to the men, we'd drive around sticking flyers in windshields. Not even typed up either, just Magic Marker, Xeroxed, "Party!"

— Jerry Seinfeld

Anything interesting in a Chicano family begins or ends in the backyard. Weddings are the best. "We're going to move all the cars out. Even that one. Rudy will get a truck from work and drag it out. We'll cut the grass, nice. The driveway, put sand on the oil, and it will be the dance floor."

— George Lopez

The divorce rate is sky high and I blame the vows. Why don't we just be honest? Instead of saying "till death do us part" let's just go, "I'll give it a shot." Or "I'm cool as long as he don't do nothing stupid."

— Wanda Sykes

My husband is very frugal, God bless him. He wanted to get married in a bank, because the videotaping is free.

— Ellen Orchid

My wife and I got into a huge argument about the wedding cake. The cake! She would ask, "How many layers? What kind of icing? These are decisions we need to be making." Finally I said, "You know, honey, I like pie. Let's have a huge wedding pie!" Suddenly I was out of the planning loop.

— Jeffrey Jena

I recently went to a wedding rehearsal. After that, the bride and groom had a marriage rehearsal: they watched TV until they fell asleep.

— Denise Munro Robb

Skimp on your wedding dress. Why spend a lot of money on something you're only going to wear five or six times?

— Charisse Savarin

I was the Best Man at a wedding. I thought the title was a bit much. If I'm the Best Man, why is she marrying him?

— Jerry Seinfeld

I love weddings, but I cry. Because they're not mine.

— Wendy Liebman

Being religious, my wife and I decided to find Bible verses for each other as part of the wedding ceremony. I chose something about being "equally yoked" for her. She chose Ephesians 6:5 for me: "Slaves, obey your earthly masters with respect and fear."

— Jeff Scott

On her wedding day, a Masai tribeswoman symbolizes her low status by putting dung on her head. American women may have to put up with a lot of bullshit, but at least we don't have to wear it.

— Jackie Wollner

My fiancé is an atheist, he believes in science, but he wants his belief system reflected in our wedding ceremony. What does that mean: Stephen Hawking will perform the ceremony? "By the power vested in me by the National Academy of Science I pronounce you an inert mass of DNA. You may exchange saliva."

— Denise Robb

My wife didn't marry me with an "I do," but with an "I guess."

— Rich Feldman

It seems like the only times they pronounce you anything in life are when they pronounce you man and wife, or dead on arrival.

— Dennis Miller

* WEIGHT *

I had this boyfriend who told me he thought I needed to lose weight. He really hurt my feelings, but he was right. I'm proud to say I lost 173 pounds, when I dumped him. I can't tell you how much better I feel.

— Wendy Kamenoff

Men date thin girls because they're too weak to argue and salads are cheap.

— Jennifer Fairbanks

I'm starting to gain a little weight because you live with a man, you gain weight. You know why? You starved your whole life to get one; you got one; you're going to eat now.

— Elayne Boosler

I'm happy to say I lost the weight after the baby. Of course, it took me four years, and we adopted.

— Andrea Henry

I'm a housewife, but I prefer to be called a Domestic Goddess.

— Roseanne Barr

Wives are people who think it's against the law not to answer the phone when it rings.

— Rita Rudner

If my wife has taught me anything, it's this: no matter what in the world I am doing, I should be doing it differently.

— Jason Love

People ask, "Are you a good cook?" No, but I'm a great wife. I married my Georgie, the first day I said, "Pick out which room in the house you want me to be great in." Thank God, he goes out to eat a lot.

— Totie Fields

* WOMEN *

I've discovered what women want most in life, and it's a fruit-scented, sparkly lotion.

— Jeff Scott

All women want from men is a partner who will share his hopes, his thoughts, his dreams. And if you don't, we're going to bitch at you until the day you die.

— **Stephanie Hodge**

Women interrogate you. You can't lie, because women are like lawyers when they ask you where you been. "So you left at 2:20, and it takes fifteen minutes to get from here to the club, it's now 5:15 in the morning—let the court show I'm about to bust your ass!"

— **Jamie Foxx**

* **YOUNGER MEN** *

I hit on a young guy the other night, but it turned out he was twenty-one. I have unfertilized eggs older than that.

— **Robin Fairbanks**

❋ GREEN ROOM ❋

A few words about the comedians

Comedian **Orny Adams** can be seen yukking it up at Gotham Comedy Club. Orny's credits include Comedy Central, *Friday Night Videos*, and the *Late Show with David Letterman*.

*

Simone Alexander is a San Francisco-based stand-up comedian and contributing writer to Laugh.com. Contact: quofacit@aol.com.

*

Comedian **Tim Allen** has been the star of the now-syndicated sitcom *Home Improvement* and movies that include *Toy Story* and *Galaxy Quest*.

*

Woody Allen is a comedian, actor, and Academy Award-winning director of films that include *Annie Hall* and *Mighty Aphrodite*.

*

Morey Amsterdam was a comedian best known for his role as a comedy writer on *The Dick Van Dyke Show*.

*

Comedian **Karen Anderson** has performed on Comedy Central and written for E! Television.

*

Lee Arleth is a stand-up comic from New Jersey. She is also a well-known masochist, as she refuses to date anyone but other comedians. This qualifies her for all the free antidepressants she can swallow at the local clinic.

Tom Arnold is a comedian and actor who has appeared in the movies, including *True Lies* and *Nine Months*.

Comedian **Joanne Astrow** has appeared on *The Tonight Show* and in the movie *Wisecracks*, and acted as co-producer for the movie *With Friends Like These*.

*

Comedian **Dave Attell** is host of Comedy Central's *Insomniac*.

*

Vinny Badabing is a writer and comedian from New Jersey. You can see more of his work at vinny-badabing.com.

*

Rosalie Bahmer's journey to the field of stand-up comedy started as a magician's assistant in the cold Arctic, which led to the loss of three toes on her left foot, and instilled in her a love of performance that could not be denied. She carries her toes around in a little jar in her purse. If she really likes you, she'll put one in your drink when you aren't looking. Oh, and she loves potatoes. Contact: rbahmer@hotmail.com.

Comedian **Michele Balan** performs all over the country, has appeared at the Montreal Comedy festival, and has released both a comedy CD and DVD. Web site: www.michelebalan.com.

*

Vicki Barbolak won California's Funniest Female Competition and has been featured as a *Jenny Jones Show* Comedy Diva. Vicki lives in a trailer in Vista California with her two daughters and dog Sparky, who bears an amazing resemblance to Suzanne Summers.

*

Comedian **Arj Barker** has starred in his own Comedy Central special. Web site: www.arjbarker.com.

*

Roseanne Barr is the comedian who has specialized in the eponymous TV shows *Roseanne* the sitcom, *The Roseanne Show* talk show, and *The Real Roseanne Show* reality show.

*

Dave Barry is the author of a bazillion humor books, including *The World According to Dave Barry*.

*

Cartoonist and novelist **Lynda Barry** is the author of books that include *The Good Times are Killing Me* and *Cruddy*.

Joy Behar is a comedian and actress who serves as comic relief on the ABC daytime talk show *The View*.

*

Jonathan Bell performs in comedy clubs throughout the Southeast, in Las Vegas, and at numerous colleges and universities. Web site: www.jonathanbellcomedy.com.

*

Doug Benson is a stand-up comedian and actor whose recent television credits include NBC's *Friends* and his own Comedy Central special. He is an agent provocateur of the hit off-Broadway show *The Marijuana-Logues*.

*

Comedian **Suzy Berger** has appeared at the Montreal Comedy Festival and her material has been featured in the book *A Funny Time to be Gay*.

*

Comedian **Karen Bergreen** has appeared on Comedy Central's *Premium Blend*.

*

Comedian **Shashi Bhatia** has appeared as a host on the Sci-Fi Channel, on the sitcoms *Friends* and *Seinfeld*, and in the movie *Leaving Las Vegas*. Contact: ShashiBhatia@hotmail.com.

Mike Binder is a comedian, screenwriter, director, and creator of the HBO series *The Mind of a Married Man*. Web site: www.mikebinder.net.

*

Former Rat Pack comedian **Joey Bishop** performed in movies that ranged from *The Naked and the Dead* in 1958 to *Mad Dog Time* in 1996.

*

Comedian **Margot Black** is a writer, producer, and stand-up comedian whose credits include MTV's *Jenny McCarthy Show* and *Late Night with David Letterman*.

*

Comedian **Christine Blackburn** is co-host of Thursday Night Funnies at the Comedy Store in Hollywood and has appeared in over 60 national commercials and infomericals. Say hi at Peaceburn@aol.com.

*

Bill Blank is a comic from Des Moines, Iowa, who performs across the U.S. and has appeared on Spike TV. Web site: www.billblank.com.

*

Comedian **Stephanie Blum** took first-prize in the Ladies of Laughter Funniest Female competition at Madison Square Garden, was chosen by HBO's US Comedy Arts Festival to be their 2003 "Breakout Performer," and also is a *Star Search* winner. Web site: www.actoneentertainment.net.

Erma Bombeck was a housewife and humorist with dozens of best-selling humor books to her credit.

*

Comedian **Elayne Boosler** has starred in her own HBO and Showtime specials, including *Party of One*, and is the host of PAX TV's *Balderdash*. Web site: www.elayneboosler.com.

*

Cathie Boruch is a stand-up comedian who has performed on *Saturday Night Live, One Life to Live*, and Showtime. Web site: www.GreerLange.com/talent/cathieboruch.

*

Sue Bova is an actress, comedian, singer, and voice-over/jingle artist for films, television, Internet radio, musical theater, and opera. Web site: http://killerreel.com/sue_bova/sue_bova.html.

*

Steve Boyer is a comedian who has performed across the United States and acted on Broadway. Web site: www.thatboyerkid.com.

*

Alicia Brandt is a stand-up comedian and an actress who has appeared in a range of roles from *General Hospital* to the movie *Mousehunt*.

*

Joanna Briley is a New York-based stand-up comedian.

Gloria Brinkworth is a psychologist and stand-up comedian who has performed at The Comedy Store.

*

Steve Brown is a firefighter and paramedic who has also performed at the Ontario, California Improv and the Comedy Store in Hollywood. Web site: www.smokeeater11@aol.com.

Maureen Brownsey is a comedian and filmmaker. Her films include *True Blue*.

*

Comedian **Lenny Bruce** is the comedian who practically invented comedy plain-speak in the second half of the twentieth century. Bruce also produced albums that include his *Carnegie Hall Concert* and wrote the book *How to Talk Dirty and Influence People*.

*

Comedian and writer **Eileen Budd** performs in New York, New Jersey, and Connecticut in clubs that include Don't Tell Mama, Rose's Turn, The Duplex, and The Triad. Contact: eileenbudd@hotmail.com.

*

Comedian **Brett Butler** has been the star of the sit-com *Grace under Fire*. Web site: www.brettbutler.com.

Comedian **Joey Callahan** has performed on Comedy Central and ESPN's *Lighter Side of Sports*. Web site: www.joeycallahan.com.

*

Comedian **George Carlin** has won a Grammy, a CableACE award, and was nominated for an Emmy for his comedy albums and HBO and network comedy specials. Web site: www.georgecarlin.com.

*

Comedian **Jim Carrey** is the star of films that range from *Dumb and Dumber* to *The Truman Show* and *Man on the Moon*.

*

Jean Carroll was a groundbreaking comedian of the 1950s, who appeared on *The Ed Sullivan Show* and many other TV programs of the period, and who also released the comedy record *Girl in the Hot Steam Bath*.

*

Johnny Carson hosted NBC's *The Tonight Show* for more than thirty years.

*

Comedian **Christopher Case** has been a writer and producer for the sitcoms *Titus* and *Reba*.

*

Tamara Castle is an actress and comedian who has appeared on Comedy Central and *The Tonight Show* and in movies that include *Pirates of the Caribbean*. Contact: copycatgrafix@sbcglobal.net.

Comedian **Jeff Cesario** has won two Emmys and six CableACE awards for writing and producing *The Larry Sanders Show*, *Dennis Miller Live*, and his own HBO and Comedy Central stand-up specials. Web site: www.jeffcesario.com.

*

Lori Chapman has been performing stand-up comedy for the last four years all over the West Coast from Seattle to San Diego. She's also single, and, at this point, she's willing to settle for less.

*

Bonnie Cheeseman does stand-up comedy because it beats sit-down sulking.

*

Comedian **Margaret Cho** is the comedy diva and star of her own stand-up films, *I'm the One That I Want*, *Notorious C.H.O.*, and *Revolution*. Web site: www.margaretcho.com.

*

Ellen Cleghorne has been a featured player on *Saturday Night Live* and her own WBN series *Cleghorne*.

*

Comedian **Jack Coen** has made a dozen appearances on *The Tonight Show* and, no fools they, they made him a staff writer. He also recently starred in his own Comedy Central special.

Jane Condon won the 2004 Ladies of Laughter Contest in the Pro Division. Web site: www.janecondon.com.

*

Scotland's favorite comedian, **Billy Connolly**, has also been featured in films, including his star turn in *Her Majesty, Mrs. Brown*. Web site: www.billyconnolly.com.

*

Troy Conrad is a Los Angeles-based comedian and actor and writer who contributed to NBC's *Last Comic Standing*. Web site: www.troyconradthemovie.com.

*

The title of his first comedy album was prophetic: **Bill Cosby** *Is a Very Funny Fellow, Right?* Which continued to be true during a forty-year career, that includes the 1984–92 TV run of *The Cosby Show*, and books such as *Fatherhood* and *Time Flies*.

*

Mike Cotayo is a comedian with a physical disability who is best known for laughing when the chips are down. Web site: funnymanmike.com.

*

Aurora Cotsbeck is an Australian actress and comedian who has also appeared on the TV series *Stingers* and *Neighbors*.

Eileen Courtney, is a former TV technical director, comedian, and current full-time mom, who is always funny, and needs to be to keep her sanity.

*

The Covert Comic is a real CIA officer who likes to write intelligence jokes and prose, and post them on his Web site. His beautiful wife is expected to let him back in the house any day now. Web site: covertcomic.com.

*

Comedian **Courtney Cronin** has been seen on HBO's *Curb Your Enthusiasm*, and is a featured writer and performer on ESPN's *Mohr Sports*.

*

Comedian **Sunda Croonquist** is a wife and mother of two daughters, and she has performed on Comedy Central, VH-1, HBO, Showtime, and Lifetime Television's *Strong Medicine*.

*

Jayson Cross is a model and a comedian. In addition to TV appearances which include MTV, VH1, and *As the World Turns*, Jayson has modeled for *Cosmopolitan* and *Playgirl*. Website: www.jaysoncross.com.

*

Comedian **Billy Crystal** has been an actor in and director of comedy movies that include *City Slickers* and *When Harry Met Sally*.

Comedian **Sara Cytron** has been featured in the PBS lesbian and gay series *In the Life* and in the book *Out Loud & Laughing*.

*

Comedian **Michael Dane** has been entertaining audiences as a stand-up comedian for fifteen years everywhere from Seattle to Maine and with his solo show *No Apparent Motive*. He also created the Gay and Lesbian Comedy Night at the Comedy Store in Hollywood.

*

Comedian **Rodney Dangerfield** starred in the movies *Caddyshack, Back to School* and improbably enough, *Natural Born Killers*, and also won a Grammy for his comedy album *No Respect*. Web site: www.rodney.com.

*

Beth Davidoff is a stand-up comedian, writer, and stay-at-home mom who lives in Las Vegas. Web site: www.comedy.com/bethd.

*

Comedian **Ellen DeGeneres** is the groundbreaking star of ABC's *Ellen*, and has been featured in movies that include *Love Letters* and *Mr. Wrong*, and on her own talk show.

Comedian **Jessica Delfino** has been a finalist on ABC *Good Morning America's* Make Us Laugh All Night Long Competition, and a writer for the MTV show I Bet You Will. Web site: jessydelfino.blogspot.com.

*

Ann Design is a stand-up comic from New York City, who has appeared in several TV commercials. Contact: anndesign@yahoo.com.

*

Comedian **Tony Deyo** performs at comedy clubs across the U.S. Web site: www.tonydeyo.com.

*

Phyllis Diller was one of the first women stand-up comedians to go professional in the 1950s, and her nearly fifty-year career included a number of movies and dozens of TV shows, including *The Tonight Show.*

*

Comedian **Frances Dilorinzo** has appeared on Comedy Central and in USO Tours around the world. Web site: www.francesd.com.

*

Comedian **Janine DiTullio** has been a staff writer for *Late Night with Conan O'Brien* and *The Jon Stewart Show.*

*

Comedian **Joe Ditzel** is also editor of the book, *Best of the Net Wits*, and his own weekly humor column is syndicated at his Web site: joeditzel.com.

Marsha Doble has been featured in the book *The Guide to Laughing at Sex*.

*

Comedian **Tom Dreesen** has performed extensively in a three-decade comedy career including in Las Vegas, on *The Tonight Show*, and as an opening act for Elvis Presley and Frank Sinatra. Web site: www.tomdreeson.com.

*

Devin Dugan is a professional comedian based in Southern California, who has also published three books, including *Texas Midnight*. Web site: www.devindugan.com.

*

Comedian **Mike Dugan** has appeared on *The Tonight Show* with Jay Leno, and won an Emmy Award for writing on HBO's *Dennis Miller: Live*. He is also the author of the one-man show *Men Fake Foreplay*. Web site: www.menfakeforeplay.com.

*

Kelli Dunham is your typical ex-nun, skateboard-riding, houseboat-dwelling stand-up comic. She recently released her debut comedy CD, somewhat defensively titled "I Am Not a 12-Year-Old Boy!" Web site: www.kellidunham.com.

*

Political comedian **Will Durst** was host of the award-winning PBS series *We Do the Work*, taped a *One Night Stand for HBO*, and starred in A&E's *A Year's Worth with Will Durst*, which was nominated for a CableACE Award. Durst also has been nominated five times for an American Comedy Award but still hasn't won, making him the Susan Lucci of stand-up. Web site: www.willdurst.com.

*

Comedian **Bil Dwyer** has appeared on most of the defunct stand-up shows, and has had guest starring roles on *The Larry Sanders Show* and *Ally McBeal*.

*

Sandy Ehlers has performed at New York Comedy Club in NYC and Florida, Gotham Comedy Club, and Comedy Cellar. Her TV credits include *The View.* Contact: SMEhlers1@aol.com.

*

Comedian **Chas Elstner** has performed at hundreds of comedy clubs including Comic Strip Live, opened for Gloria Estefan, and appeared on MTV and Showtime.

*

Lynn Epstein is a California comedian who has appeared at the Comedy Store and the Improv in Hollywood. Check her out at http://home.earthlink.net/~lynnsfunny/.

*

Comedian **Bob Ettinger** has appeared on *Evening at the Improv* and Showtime's *Comedy Club Network*.

*

Leah Eva is a San Francisco-based stand-up comedian who tells us she also hopes to be the first Filipina-American to have more shoes than Imelda Marcos. Contact: leahsmillions@aol.com.

Comedian **Jennifer Fairbanks** has performed on UPN's *Vibe* and is a member of the comedy troupe Fresh Meat, an award-winning San Francisco improv group.

*

Robin Fairbanks is the co-founder of the Seattle female comedian shows Material Girls and The Divine Order of the Ha Ha Sisterhood, and performs in clubs across the U.S. Web site: www.robinfairbank.com.

*

Michael Feldman has been featured in the book *That's Funny.*

*

Rich Feldman is a stand-up comedian who lives in Queens, and is a new father. "That's all you need to know, and quite frankly, that's all there is. Except, oh yeah, I eat too much." Contact: rgfeld@yahoo.com.

*

What a frigging coincidence—**Craig Ferguson** is the host of the CBS *Late Late Show with Craig Ferguson.*

*

Tina Fey is the anchor of *Saturday Night Live's* Weekend Update and screenwriter of the movie *Mean Girls.*

*

Totie Fields was one of the top women comedians of the 1950s, and her television appearances included *The Ed Sullivan Show* and *The Tonight Show.*

Mel Fine is a working comedian throughout the Midwest, and the winner of the Indianapolis Funniest Person Contest.

*

Carrie Fisher is an actress and writer known for the *Star Wars* trilogy, and for her best-selling books *Postcards from the Edge*, *Surrender the Pink*, and *Delusions of Grandma*.

*

Comedian **Diane Ford** has received eight nominations for an American Comedy Award. Her HBO specials are classics.

*

Comedian **Karith Foster** has performed on VH1, Comedy Central's *Premium Blend*, Bravo, and *Showtime at the Apollo*. Contact: karith@hotmail.com.

*

Comedian **Jeff Foxworthy** is known both for his former eponymous sitcom and *You Might Be a Redneck If*, "the biggest-selling comedy album of all time." Foxworthy recently released a new CD, *Big Funny*, and hosts Comedy Central's *Blue Collar Comedy*. Web site: www.jefffoxworthy.com.

*

TV star turned screen actor **Jamie Foxx** first became known for his many roles on the comedy variety show *In Living Color*. Since then, Foxx has earned particular acclaim for his roles in *Any Given Sunday* and as Ray Charles in the Oscar-winning *Ray*.

Comedian **Catherine Franco** has played leading ladies in heavy theatrical shows such as *Extremities* and *Children of a Lesser God*, played home-wrecking bitches in a dozen soap operas, and now performs in comedy clubs that include the Laugh Factory in Los Angeles. Contact: cbocaloca@aol.com.

*

Sir David Frost has been in the front line of television news and entertainment for over forty years beginning with the satirical news program *That Was The Week That Was* on the BBC in 1962, which was followed by a variety of interview programs in the UK and America, broadcast all round the world.

*

Comedian **Caryl Fuller's** book and solo show, *Dueling Hearts*, is a comic tour de force about charming men and the rollercoaster ride of romance. Contact: carylfuller@aol.com.

*

Douglas Gale is originally from a town in New Hampshire you've never heard of, and is currently a stand-up comic in Seattle. Contact: the_dgale@hotmail.com.

*

Comedian **Zach Galifianakis** has been a writer for *That '70s Show* and appeared in movies including *Corky Romano*.

*

Mary Gallagher is an actress and comedian whose television credits include *Friends* and *The Tonight Show*. Web site: www.marygallagher.tv.

Janeane Garofalo is the queen of the alternative comedians and an actress who has appeared in films that include *The Truth about Cats and Dogs* and *Mystery Men*, as well as serving as a talk show host for Air America Radio.

*

Comedian **Emmy Gay** has appeared at venues that include both the Apollo Theater and the Joseph Papp Public Theater. Web site: www.emmygay.com.

*

Larry Getlen is a New York-based comedian, journalist, and actor who has written for *Esquire* magazine and Comedy Central's *Tough Crowd with Colin Quinn*, and appeared on *Chappelle's Show*. Web site: www.zhet.blogspot.com.

*

Lori Giarnella is making a name for herself in her hometown of Pittsburgh, Pennsylvania. Web site: laughwithlori.com.

*

Johnnye Jones Gibson works for a newspaper, freelances as a journalist, writes screenplays, and travels the world interviewing and writing newsletters for Anthony Robbins Seminars and other events.

Irv Gilman is a comedian, MC, and former Council Member of Monterey Park, California.

*

Comedian **Joy Gohring** has appeared on Comedy Central and *The Late Late Show with Craig Kilborn*.

Comedian **Judy Gold** has appeared on HBO's *Comic Relief, The Tonight Show*, and starred in her own Comedy Central special. Web site: www.judygold.com.

*

Comedian **Bob Goldthwait** has starred in the movie *Scrooged* and on TV series that include *Unhappily Ever After*. Bob has also directed his movie *Shakes the Clown*, and *Chapelle's Show* on Comedy Central.

*

Comedian **Mimi Gonzalez** produced the weekly stand-up show Women with Balls for six years in Los Angeles and San Francisco. Mimi has also performed comedy from Wenatchee to Biloxi to Tallahasee to Albany, and counts entertaining the troops in Japan, Korea, Bosnia, and Kosovo as some of her most rewarding work. Web site: www.mimigonzalez.com.

*

Reno Goodale is a touring comedian, writer, and actor, who has written material for Jay Leno and performed as the opening act for Joan Rivers.

*

Author and comedian **Debbie Sue Goodman** performs a one-woman show based on her humorous book, *Still Single*. Web site: www.skokienet.org/goodman1.

*

Comedian **Monica Grant** is one of the hottest tickets on the women's concert circuit.

Comedian **E. L. Greggory** is a regular at the Comedy Store in Hollywood.

*

Comedian **Kathy Griffin** is the star of her own reality show *My Life on the D List* and has also been featured in the sitcom *Suddenly Susan* and movies that include *The Cable Guy* and *Pulp Fiction*. Web site: www.kathy-griffin.com.

*

Cartoonist and writer **Matt Groening** is the creator of *The Simpsons*.

*

Comedian **Debi Gutierrez** has appeared on Lifetime, Showtime, ABC's *Laughin' Out Loud*, the Just for Laughs Comedy Festival in Montreal, and the US Comedy Arts Festival in Aspen, Colorado. Web site: www.mommycomic.com.

*

Comedian **Karen Haber** has been featured on the *Arsenio Hall Show* and *Evening at the Improv* and in the video *The Girls of the Comedy Store*.

*

San Francisco comedian **Jennifer Hahamian** has been a finalist at the Improv's Battle of the Bay Comedy Competition. Contact: jhahamian@hotmail.com.

*

Comedian **Rhonda Hansome** has opened for James Brown, the Pointer Sisters, and Anita Baker, and has appeared in the film *Pretty Woman*.

Deric Harrington is a comedian who likes his Web site, dericharrington.com. He also likes the taste of victory.

*

Comedian **Lynn Harris** has written for *The New York Times, Entertainment Weekly*, and created BreakupGirl.com and three resulting books, including *Breakup Girl to the Rescue!*

Paulara R. Hawkins has been a semi-finalist in Comedy Central's Laugh Riot Competition, and been featured as one of the Comedians to Watch on *The Jenny Jones Show*. Web site: www.artistWeb site.com/paularapage.html.

*

Comedian **Laura Hayden** has been featured at the Boston International Comedy Festival, and has been a semi-finalist in the California's Funniest Female Contest. Web site: www.laurahayden.com.

*

Comedian **Mitch Hedberg** has performed on *That '70s Show* and in his own stand-up special on Comedy Central. Web site: www.mitchhedberg.net.

*

John Heffron has been the winning comedian and last comic standing on the second season of NBC's Last Comic Standing. Web site: www.johnheffron.com.

Janice J. Heiss is a writer and recovering stand-up comedian who lives and laughs in San Francisco. Contact: jjheiss@yahoo.com.

*

Kevin Hench, TV producer and comedy writer, is supervising producer of *The Sports List* on Fox Sports Net.

Andrea Henry is a Greek-American comic from Boston, who thanks her family for the infinite material. Web site: www.andreahenry.com.

*

Comedian **Carol Henry** has been featured in HBO's *Women of the Night III*.

*

Tom Hertz has been a featured patient on Comedy Central's *Dr. Katz, Professional Therapist*.

*

Comedian **Rene Hicks** starred in her own Comedy Central special, appeared in the movie *Low, Down Dirty Shame* and has been nominated for an American Comedy Award. Web site: www.renehicks.com.

*

Comedian **Stephanie Hodge** starred in the syndicated sitcom *Unhappily Ever After*.

Comedian **Steve Hofstetter** is the author of the *Student Body Shots* series, available at bookstores everywhere. Web site: www.stevehofstetter.com.

*

Daryl Hogue is a comedian and voiceover talent whose clients include 7-11, Ford, and Hewlett Packard. She performs in clubs in the Los Angeles area.

*

Comedian **Corey Holcomb** has been a finalist on NBC's *Last Comic Standing*.

*

Geoff Holtzman is a comedian and writer living somewhere on the East Coast, who can be contacted at geoffholtzman@yahoo.com.

*

Tim Homayoon has written for *Saturday Night Live* and headlines in comedy clubs across the U.S. Web site: www.thatcomedyguy.com.

*

Comedian **Maryellen Hooper** won an American Comedy Award. Her numerous television appearances include *The Tonight Show*, and her own Comedy Central special. Web site: www.maryellenhooper.com

*

Bob Hope was a comedian whose career ranged over seven decades from vaudeville to a series of *Road* movies with Bing Crosby and innumerable television specials.

Comedian **Alex House** has appeared on *Last Comic Standing* and *The View*. She has twice won the Bud Light Ladies of Laughter contest. Web site: www.comedy.com/alexhouse.

*

Christina Irene has dreamt of becoming a professional writer since she was seven years old, and her comedy career is a fulfillment of that dream. Web site: www.christinairene.com.

*

Comedian **Dom Irrera** has starred in his own HBO specials and also appeared on TV shows that include *Everybody Loves Raymond* and *The Drew Carey Show* and movies that include *The Big Lebowski*.

*

Jeffrey Jena is a writer and stand-up comic who has appeared on over thirty national television shows. Jeff is also a regular guest on Bob and Tom Radio. Web site: JeffreyJena.com.

*

Comedian **Jenée** has performed stand-up around the globe, including USO tours of Korea, Bosnia, and Kosovo. Jenée is also a regular contributor to *US Magazine*'s Fashion Police. Web site: www.jenee.net.

*

Comedian **Richard Jeni** has been rewarded for his comic fluidity with two CableACE Awards and one American Comedy Award. Web site: www.richardjeni.com.

Comedian **Chuck Johnson** has performed at the Palos Verdes Players Theater.

*

Comedian **Jenny Jones** has also been the host of *The Jenny Jones Show*. Web site: www.jennyjones.com.

*

Comedian **Diana Jordan** has been nominated for an American Comedy Awards, has appeared in the movie *Jerry McGuire*, and is a co-author of the book *Women are from Venus, Men are from Uranus*. Website: www.dianajordan.com.

*

Comedian **Norman K.** performs in clubs in the New York area. Contact: normank_comic@hotmail.com.

*

Comedian **Cory Kahaney** was a finalist in the first season of NBC's *Last Comic Standing* and has also appeared on Lifetime's *Girl's Night Out*, NBC's *Comedy Showcase*, and Comedy Central.

*

Wendy Kamenoff is a comedian whose first book, *You've Got Meal*, is an email diary about food and body image. Web site: www.wendykamenoff.com.

*

Comedian **Jann Karam** has appeared on *Politically Incorrect*, *The Tonight Show*, *Evening at the Improv*, and Lifetime's *Girls Night Out*. Web site: www.jannkaram.com.

Stand-up comedian and two-time Emmy-nominated writer **Debbie Kasper** is the co-writer and co-star of the play *Venus Attacks!* a parody of self-help seminars. Web site: www.debbiekasper.org.

*

Comedian **Jonathan Katz** played doctor on Comedy Central's *Dr. Katz, Professional Therapist* and is the author of the book *To Do Lists of the Dead*.

*

Comedian **Sheila Kay** has been nominated for an American Comedy Award and is currently touring in *Venus Attacks*, a comedy about love, sex and self-help. Web site: www.venusattacks.org.

*

Comedian **Martha Kelly** has appeared on Comedy Central, and is one of the comedians featured in the first season of NBC's *Last Comic Standing*.

*

Comedian **Bobby Kelton** has appeared on *The Tonight Show* and *The Late Show with David Letterman*.

*

Jen Kerwin has been featured in NBC's *Last Comic Standing*.

*

Comedian **Julie Kidd** has been featured on NBC's *Power of Laughter* and on ABC's *The View*, where Joy Behar said of her, "Julie Kidd is one of the funniest housewives in America!" Check her out at www.funnysinglemom.com.

Comedian **Laura Kightlinger** has also been a writer and producer of the sitcom *Will and Grace*.

*

Comedian **Craig Kilborn** has been the host of CBS's *The Late Late Show*.

*

Comedian **Brian Kiley** is an Emmy-nominated writer who appears regularly on *The Tonight Show* and *Late Night with Conan O'Brien*.

*

Matze Knop is a DJ on Radio NRW, Europe's largest syndicated radio station. Matze has also performed extensively on German TV stations, including RTL, Sat1 and NBC Europe, and hosted his own cable comedy show from 2002 to 2004. Web site: www.matzeknop.de.

*

After graduating from Northwestern University in 2001, comedian **Dava Krause** moved to Los Angeles, where she has become a regular performer at The Comedy Store. Web site: www.davakrause.com.

*

Comedian **Cathy Ladman** has appeared on *The Tonight Show* a bazillion times, has played a recurring character on the sitcom *Caroline in the City*, and also appeared on the now-syndicated sitcom *Just Shoot Me*.

Maura Lake is an actress and comedian who has appeared on *Days of Our Lives* and *The Bold and the Beautiful*. She is also a graduate of the Groundlings Theater.

*

Comedian **Beth Lapides** is the creator of the Uncabaret, and has performed in and produced the Uncabaret touring company, a Comedy Central special, and a CD. Check her out at www.uncabaret.com.

*

Comedian **Thyra Lees-Smith** lives in Los Angeles and performs in many local clubs, including the Improv and the Comedy Store.

*

Comedian **Carol Leifer** has been a producer on *Seinfeld*, the star of her own sitcom *Alright Already*, and is a judge on the new *Star Search*.

*

Comedian **LeMaire** has appeared on the *Caroline Rhea Show*, *The Tonight Show*, and Comedy Central's *Make Me Laugh*.

*

Mike Lemme is a comedian from Chicopee, Massachusetts, who can be reached atellemmeo@yahoo.com.

*

Comedian **Jay Leno** is the host of NBC's *The Tonight Show*.

Comedian **David Letterman** is the host of CBS's *Late Show*.

*

Comedian **Emily Levine** has been a television writer for series that include *Designing Women*, and although this ain't much of a segue, a subsequent invitation to a physicists' think tank resulted in her one-woman show, *eLevine.universe*, synthesizing comedy and philosophy.

*

In addition to his numerous HBO specials, comedian **Richard Lewis** has starred in the sitcom *Anything But Love*, and in the Mel Brooks movie *Robin Hood: Men in Tights*. www.richardlewisonline.com.

*

Daniel Liebert is one of the top freelance joke writers in the U.S. He marches to the same god-damn drummer everyone else does. Contact: DLiebert@msn.com.

*

Comedian **Wendy Liebman** has appeared on *The Tonight Show*, in her own HBO comedy special, and has won an American Comedy Award. Web site: www.wendyliebman.com.

*

Shirley Lipner is a comedian who has also been the warm-up for the TBN shows *Rocky Road, Safe at Home*, and *Down To Earth*.

Comedian **Penelope Lombard** tours clubs and colleges around the country, and has been seen in numerous TV appearances including on Comedy Central.

*

Comedian **George Lopez** is the star of the *George Lopez* show on ABC. Web site: www.georgelopez.com.

*

Comedian **Leighann Lord** has appeared on Comedy Central's *Premium Blend*, NBC's *Comedy Showcase*, and ABC's *The View*. Leighann has won the Best Actress award in The Riant Theatre Play Festival for her one woman show, *The Full Swanky*, and also won the New York City Black Comedy Award as the Most Thought-Provoking Female Comic. Web site: www.leighannlord.com.

*

Susie Loucks has appeared on A&E's *Evening at the Improv, Caroline's Comedy Hour*, and on an impressive number of other comedy shows.

*

Jason Love is a stand-up comedian whose cartoon *Snapshots* has garnered a worldwide audience through syndication in thirty-two newspapers, dozens of magazines, 500 Web sites, and a line of greeting cards. Web site: www.jasonlove.com.

*

Marla Lukofsky is a twenty-year Canadian comedy veteran and voice-over artist.

Mari Lund is an actress and comedian who has performed at clubs which include the Hollywood Improv and The Comedy Store. Web site: www.marilund.biz.

*

Carmen Lynch has appeared on Comedy Central and *The Tonight Show*.

*

In a career that spanned fifty years, **Moms Mabley's** comedy performances ranged from the Cotton Club and the Apollo Theater to Carnegie Hall. Moms also recorded nine very popular comedy albums for Chess Records in the 1960s.

*

Tracey MacDonald is the first Canadian female stand-up comedian to become a Star Search Grand Champion. Web site: www.traceymacdonald.com.

*

Comedian **Kathleen Madigan** won an American Comedy Award for Best Female Stand-up and starred in her very own HBO *Comedy Half Hour*. Her album *Kathleen Madigan* is available from Uproar Entertainment. Web site: www.kathleenmadigan.com.

*

Kelly Maguire is an actress and comedian who has performed at the Comedy Store and the Improv in Hollywood, participated in the Aspen Comedy Festival, and won a Dramalogue award for Best Actress. Her recent film credits include *Stranger in my House* for Lifetime television.

Meg Maly and her partner **Blamo Risher** are one of the few male-female stand-up comedy teams in America. Web site: www.funnysincebirth.com.

*

Liisa Mannerkoski is an actress and comedian who has performed at the Improv in Hollywood. Web site: www.liisamannerkoski.com.

*

Steve Martin is a comedian who has starred in, written, and directed comedy films that include *The Jerk* and *Bowfinger*.

*

Comedian **Monique Marvez's** signature raunchy wit and sexualized sarcasm is showcased on her CD, *Built for Comfort*. Web site: www.moniquemarvez.com.

*

Groucho Marx was a comedian who, with The Marx Brothers, made a number of the funniest films of the 1930s, including *Duck Soup*, and whose marvelous 1950s game show, *You Bet Your Life*, still deserves viewing on some cable channel smart enough to feature it.

*

Jackie Mason is a forty-year comedy veteran, and the star of several one-man Broadway shows, including *The World According to Me*. Web site: www.jackiemason.com.

Kate Mason is a comedian who plays clubs and colleges everywhere.

*

Comedian **Denise McCanles** is also a reporter for *LesbiaNation* and has appeared on the syndicated TV show *Night Stand*.

*

Comedian **Laurie McDermott** has appeared all over Australia, London, and New Zealand. Laurie has been seen on dozens of commercials and international television shows, and is a humor columnist for *Bride Magazine*. Web site: www.lauriemcdermott.com.

*

Bonnie McFarlane is a Canadian comedian who has played at Yuk Yuks comedy club.

*

Comedian **Kris McGaha** is the Excess Hollywood Correspondent on NBC's *Tonight Show*, and has also appeared in NBC's *Comedy Showcase*, on HBO's *Curb Your Enthusiasm* and in the film, *Following Tildy*. Web site: www.krismcgaha.com.

*

Paul McGinty has been an actor, a comedy radio show host, a stand-up comic, and a cut-up at the dinner table as a kid.

*

Brian McKim is a writer and a stand-up comedian who is also the editor and publisher of SHECKYmagazine.com.

Comedian **John Mendoza** has appeared on *The Tonight Show* and was one of Showtime's *Pair of Jokers.*

*

Maria Menozzi is a writer, actress, and stand-up comedian who performs across the country. She is also the author of an award-winning children's play, "The Poet Who Wouldn't Be King." Web site: www.ironuterus.com.

*

Comedian **Felicia Michaels** has won an American Comedy Award and has released her own CD *Lewd Awakenings.* Web site: www.feliciamichaels.com.

*

Cathryn Michon is a stand-up comedian who has been featured at the Montreal Comedy Festival. Cathryn has also written for a number of TV series, and is author of the books *The Grrl Genius Guide to Life,* and *The Grrl Genuis Guide to Sex.* Web site: grrlgenius.com.

*

Comedian **Beverly Mickins** has also appeared on Lifetime's *Girls Night Out, Thirtysomething,* and in the movie *Steel and Lace.*

*

Comedian **Dennis Miller** is the possessor of God-given sarcasm, but unfortunately, has gone over to the dark side as the reactionary host of CNBC's *Dennis Miller.*

Comedian **Larry Miller** is featured in both of the *Nutty Professor* movies and has played the pregnancy-obsessed father of teenagers in *Ten Things I Hate About You*.

*

Anita Milner is a lawyer, stand-up comedian and keynote speaker who enrolled in law school in her forties, passed the California Bar Exam at age fifty, and celebrated her sixtieth birthday by performing stand-up comedy in Debbie Reynolds' lounge show in Las Vegas.

*

Comedian **Modi** has appeared on HBO's *The Sopranos* and Comedy Central's *USO Tour Live from Guantanamo Bay, Cuba*. Web site: http://modi.cc/bio.html.

*

Comedian **Carol Montgomery** has appeared on *Evening at the Improv*, Showtime's *Comedy Club Network*, and *Girls Night Out*. Carol is currently featured in the live Las Vegas show, *Crazy Girls* at the Riviera Hotel and Casino.

*

Comedian **Lynda Montgomery** has appeared on VH-1's Spotlight, but considers the highlight of her career to be her performance at the 1993 March on Washington in front of an audience of an estimated one million people.

Comedian **Tonya Moon** performs at the Comedy Store in the Ding-Dong Show. Web site: www.thedingdongshow.com.

*

Comedian **Maureen Murphy** has appeared on *The Tonight Show* and in the *Girls of the Comedy Store* video.

Robert Murray performs at various venues around Southern California. Contact: robcmurray@hotmail.com.

*

Rebecca Nell is an actress, writer, and comedian who has performed at a number of Los Angeles clubs, including the Comedy Store.

*

In addition to stand-up, **Jackie Newton** has also been a keynote speaker for the state International Reading Association meetings for Missouri, and has developed a K-12 assembly program for schools, Youth Against Violence. Web site: www.jackienewton.com.

*

Comedian **Diane Nichols** has been named "a Queen of Comedy" and "the heroine of the 9 to 5 crowd" by *Newsweek*.

Buzz Nutley is a professional comedian who has written for the *Pittsburgh Post Gazette* and *Los Angeles Times*, has sold material to Jay Leno and Yakov Smirnoff, and has performed as the opening for Jon Stewart. Web site: www.buzznutley.com.

*

JeanAnn O'Brien is a stand-up comic from Seattle, Washington, who produces the Divine Order of the Ha Ha Sisterhood comedy show. Web site: laughterville.com.

*

Comedian **Rosie O'Donnell** has hosted her own cheery talk show, and been featured in movies that include *Sleepless in Seattle* and *Exit to Eden*.

*

Despite her humble origins in the Rubber Capital of Akron, Ohio, comedian **Ann Oelschlager** has risen to great success in the City of Angels, where she lives in an apartment building with a swimming pool.

*

Irish comedian **Owen O'Neill** has performed at the Montreal Comedy Festival and has been a guest on *Late Night with Conan O'Brien.*

*

Ellen Orchid is a comedian/actress/MD/psychiatrist who has been seen on *The View, Saturday Night Live, America's Funniest People, Last Comic Standing,* and *The Sopranos*. Web site: www.funnyshrink.com.

Christine O'Rourke is a screenwriter and comedian who has performed at the Improv in Hollywood.

*

Cheri Oteri has been a cast member of *Saturday Night Live* and has appeared in films that include *Scary Movie* and *Liar Liar*.

*

Tom Parks has been making people laugh for over 20 years including on *The Tonight Show*, *Late Night with David Letterman*, on both HBO and Showtime. For two seasons was the anchorman on HBO's *Not Necessarily the News* for which he was nominated for an ACE Award. Tom most recently hosted the Family Channel show, *Wait Till You Have Kids*.

*

Comedian **Nancy Patterson** has performed at Standford & Son's Comedy House, the Cleveland Improv, Bocanuts in Boca Raton, Florida, and at the Cabaret Dada improvisational theater.

*

Dave Pavone is a stand-up comedian and comedy writer based in Phoenix, Arizona. He is the co-creator of "The Timmy Sketch Project," a local comedy sketch show. Contact: dbpavone@yahoo.com.

*

Minnie Pearl, a member of the Grand Ole Opry, cast from 1940 until her death in 1996, was country music's preeminent comedian.

Comedian **Dina Pearlman** has appeared on Comedy Central's *Premium Blend* and on HBO's *Sex and the City*.

*

Elaine Pelino is a former Miss Texas and current stand-up comedian living in Los Angeles. Contact: chasebear@adelphia.net.

*

Tamara Pennington is a stand-up comic and free-lance writer, who has appeared on the TV sitcom *Friends* and in a number of independent films. Web site: www.tamarapennington.com.

Mary Pfeiffer is a self-described squeaky clean comedian. Contact: MerryPfeiffer@webtv.net.

*

Comedian **Emo Philips** has appeared on numerous HBO and Showtime specials, as well as in the "Weird" Al Yankovich movie *UHF*. Web site: www.emophilips.com.

*

Comedian **Monica Piper** won a Golden Globe for her writing on the sitcom *Roseanne* and her Showtime special *Monica, Just You* was nominated for a CableACE award.

*

Stephanie Piro is a humorist whose cartoons *Six Chix* and *Fair Game* appear in daily and weekly newspapers around the country. Web site: www.stephaniepiro.com.

Katherine Poehlmann also has a serious side as a health author and lecturer. Web site: www.RA-Infection-Connection.com.

*

Stacey Prussman is an actress and stand-up comedian who tours throughout the U.S. and Canada. She has appeared on both the Howard Stern and Ricki Lake shows. Web site: www.staceyprussman.com.

*

Comedian **Richard Pryor** is a nearly forty-year veteran of comedy recording, movies and TV, including the ground-breaking 1970s *Richard Pryor Show*, and the movie *Silver Streak*. Web site: www.richardpryor.com.

*

Comedian **Chantel Rae** has appeared on the *Best Damn Sports Show Period* and Comedy Central. Web site: chantelrae.com.

*

Comedian **Alex Reed** has performed on *Evening at the Improv.*

*

Comedian **Dennis Regan** has appeared on *The Late Show with David Letterman* and *The Tonight Show with Jay Leno.*

*

Lewis Ramey has appeared on Comedy Central's *Premium Blend.*

Melanie Reno has appeared on Comedy Central's *Premium Blend*. Check her out at www.melaniereno.com.

*

Comedian **Rick Reynolds**, whose one-man comedy show *Only the Truth is Funny* became a Showtime special, has written a follow up one-man show, *All Grown Up and No Place to Go*.

*

Comedian **Caroline Rhea** has starred on *Sabrina the Teenage Witch* and, call out the coincidence police, has also been the host of *The Caroline Rhea Show*. Web site: www.carolinerhea.com.

*

Andi Rhoads is a Los Angeles comedian who has performed at The Improv and the Comedy Store in Hollywood. Contact: andirhoads@yahoo.com.

*

Comedian **Ron Richards** won an Emmy Award for his writing on *Late Night with David Letterman*, and a CableACE Award for HBO's *Not Necessarily the News*. He has also been on the writing staff of *The Tonight Show* and NBC's *Saturday Night Live*.

*

Comedian **Adam Richmond** has appeared on Nickelodeon, Fox Sports Net, and in several national commercials. He has been a staff writer for the Canadian animated series *Chilly Beach*. Contact: gunnyfuy@yahoo.com.

Comedian **Karen Ripley** has been performing as an out lesbian since 1977 and has appeared on Comedy Central's *The Daily Show*. Web site: www.karenripley.com.

*

Joan Rivers is a comedian whose career stretches over four decades. She is also an actress, talk show host, best-selling author, and commentator for *E! Style*. Web site: www.joanrivers.com.

*

Denise Munro Robb has performed on Lifetime, A&E, Comedy Central, and MTV, and had the distinction of being the warm-up for the Los Angeles mayoral debates on CBS in 2005. She is currently at work on her Ph.D. in political science at UC Irvine because politics is so hilarious. Web site: DeniseMunroRobb.com.

*

Robin Roberts hosts and produces the critically acclaimed Los Angeles stand-up show "Comedy Schmomedy." Her satirical songs have been featured on the CDs *Stand Up Against Domestic Violence I & II*. Web site: comedyschmomedy.com.

*

Chris Rock is a comedian and actor who has been, natch, host of HBO's *The Chris Rock Show*. He has also starred in movies including the *Lethal Weapon* series, and his own concerts on CD and DVDs, including *Bigger and Blacker*.

Comedian **Roberta Rockwell** has been featured in the Toyota Comedy Festival, the Bud Light Ladies of Laughter, and has been a semi-finalist in the Gilda's Club Laugh-Off. Web site: www.robertarockwell.com.

*

Comedian **Ray Romano** starred in the CBS series *Everybody Loves Raymond*, and is the author of the best-selling book *Everything, and a Kite*. Web site: www.rayromano.com.

Janet Rosen has been featured in the New York City female comedy showcase "If We Were Men, We'd Be Famous" and the Marshall's Women in Comedy Festival. She has also written for *Glamour* and other national magazines. Contact: jrosen10@nyc.rr.com.

*

Helen Rowland was a writer and humorist whose books included *A Guide to Men*.

*

Comedian **Rita Rudner** has appeared on *The Tonight Show*, has been featured on any number of comedy specials, including her own on HBO, and is author of the books *Naked Beneath My Clothes* and *Tickled Pink*. Web site: www.ritafunny.com.

Acting, dancing, and singing her way into the hearts of millions from coast to coast, comedian **Emily Rush** can be contacted at emilyshines@hotmail.com to inquire about her book of adventures for the past ten years.

*

Comedian **Betsy Salkind** has been a writer for the now syndicated sitcom *Roseanne* and has appeared on *Arli$$* and *The Tonight Show*. Web site: www.betsysalkind.com.

*

Comedian **Adam Sandler** is a former cast member of NBC's *Saturday Night Live* and the star of a string of comedy movies, including *Happy Gilmore, The Waterboy,* and *The Wedding Singer*. Web site: www.adamsandler.com.

*

Comedian **Peter Sasso** performs in comedy clubs and on cruise ships. Contact: sassopeter@hotmail.com.

*

Comedian **Drake Sather** wrote for a number of TV shows, including *News Radio, The Dennis Miller Show,* and *Ed*, received an Emmy nomination for his work on *The Larry Sanders Show*, and co-wrote the movie *Zoolander* with actor Ben Stiller.

*

Comedian **Charisse Savarin** has appeared on *Girls Behaving Badly* on the Oxygen Network and *The Best Damn Sports Show Period*. Contact: comedy4u@comcast.net.

Comedian **Mark Schiff** is a regular performer on the *Tonight Show* and *Late Show with David Letterman* and has starred in his own Showtime special, *My Crummy Childhood.*

*

Comedian **Robert Schimmel** has been featured in his own HBO Special and his CDs include, *If You Buy This CD, I Can Buy This Car, Robert Schimmel Comes Clean,* and *Unprotected.*
Web site: www.robertschimmel.com.

*

Sue Schwartz is a comedy writer and performer living in New Jersey. Contact: mitten1992@aol.com.

*

Barbara Scott has been performing improvisation for twenty years and teaching for twelve years. She is currently a member of the acclaimed improv theatre ensemble True Fiction Magazine.

*

Jeff Scott is an up-and-coming comedian performing at local clubs in Cleveland, Ohio, including the Improv. Contact: Jeffrey_L_Scott@KeyBank.com.

*

Comedian **Jerry Seinfeld** helped rethink the sitcom with his eponymous sitcom *Seinfeld.*

Sandi Selvi is a wife and mother who triumphed over Multiple Sclerosis and a comedian who performs extensively in the San Francisco area and at The Improv in San Jose. Check her out: www.sandiselvi.com.

*

Ronnie Shakes was a comedian and TV writer who made frequent appearances on *The Tonight Show*.

*

Comedian **Garry Shandling** is the star and creator of *The Larry Sanders Show*.

*

Craig Sharf is a comedian and comedy writer who has sold material to professional comedians, including Joan Rivers, and to other comedy outlets such as the *Weinerville* TV show. Web site: www.craigsharf.com.

*

Jeff Shaw is a comedian, humor columnist, and staff writer in the Alternative Cards department of Cleveland's American Greetings Corporation. Contact: Dork2Dude@aol.com.

*

Comedian **Craig Shoemaker**'s CDs *Shoemaker Meets the Lovemaster* and *Son of the Lovemaster* morphed into writing, directing, and starring in his movie *The Lovemaster*. Craig is also the creator of the non-profit foundation Laughter Heals. Web site: www.laughterheals.com.

Comedian **Jimmy Shubert** was featured at the Just for Laughs Montreal Comedy Festival and featured in the movies *GO, Coyoye Ugly*, and *The Italian Job*. Web site: jimmyshubert.com.

*

John David Sidley is a stand-up comedian, comedy writer, and comedy teacher who lives in Cleveland, Ohio. He also performs in the comedy team of Bengston and Sidley. Web site: www.clevelandcomedy.com.

*

Comedian **Jennifer Siegal** has also worked as a Disneyland portrait artist, dot.com illustrator, movie critic, and writes a monthly art column in San Francisco. On weekends, she likes to go where the green lights take her.

*

Comedian **Sarah Silverman** has appeared in movies that include *Something About Mary* and *School of Rock*, played a comedy writer on HBO's *Larry Sanders Show,* and has been a comedy writer for *Saturday Night Live*.

*

Comedian **Sinbad** has starred in several of his own HBO specials including *Son of a Preacher Man*, and in a number of movies, including *House Guest* and *First Kid*.

Comedian **Carol Siskind** has appeared on *Evening at the Improv*, *Comic Strip Live*, *Girls Night Out*, and innumerable other comedy specials.

*

Comedian **Red Skelton** started as a vaudeville performer and worked his way up to *The Red Skelton Show*, which ran on TV for twenty years, from 1951–71.

*

Comedian **Traci Skene** is also the co-creator, editor, and publisher of www.sheckymagazine.com.

*

Bobby Slayton, the self-proclaimed "Pit Bull of Comedy" has also played "Joey Bishop" in the HBO original movie *The Rat Pack*, and appeared in the films *Get Shorty*, *Ed Wood*, and *Wayne's World 2*. Website: www.bobbyslayton.com.

*

Comedian **Bruce Smirnoff**'s award-winning one-man show is titled *Other Than My Health, I Have Nothing...And Today I Don't Feel So Good*.

*

Bob Smith, the first openly gay comic to perform on *The Tonight Show*, is also the author of the books *Way to Go, Smith*, and *Openly Bob*. Web site: http://literati.net/Smith/.

Comedian **Margaret Smith** has won an American Comedy Award, has been featured in her own Comedy Central special, and has starred in *That '80s Show*.

*

Canadian comedian **Steve Smith** is also a writer, producer, and past recipient of the Banff Television Festival's Sir Peter Ustinov Comedy Network Award.

*

Comedian **Tracy Smith** has appeared on MTV's *Half Hour Comedy Hour* and Lifetime's *Girls Night Out*.

*

Carrie Snow is a stand-up comedian who has also been a writer on the first two of the *Roseanne* TV shows.

*

Comedian **David Spade** is a star of the sitcom *Eight Rules for Dating My Teenage Daughter* and movies including *Lost and Found*. Web site: davidspade.com.

*

Comedian **Livia Squires** has appeared on Showtime, been a finalist in California's Funniest Female contest, and appears regularly at the Ice House in Pasadena. Web site: roadcomic.com.

*

Comedian **Skip Stephenson** was one of the hosts of the 1980's TV show *Real People*.

Comedian **Jon Stewart** is the host of Comedy Central's *The Daily Show*.

*

Comedian **Jeff Stilson** has been a writer for *Late Night with David Letterman* and a producer for both MTV's *The Osbournes* and HBO's *The Chris Rock Show*.

*

Comedian **Pam Stone** had a recurring role on the ABC's hit series *Coach*, has appeared in her own Showtime Special, and is winner of the Gracie Allen Award from the American Women in Radio and Television for her syndicated radio program *The Pam Stone Show*.

*

Comedian **Lisa Sunstedt** has been a featured performer in the Montreal Just for Laughs Festival, and a guest star of *Tracy Takes On*.

*

Comedian **Wanda Sykes** has been the host of Comedy Central's *Premium Blend* and star of her own sitcom *Wanda*. Web site: www.wandasykes.com.

*

Joanne Syrigonakis's comedy deals with family, divorce, and dating, and she performs at the Comedy Cabaret chain of clubs. Contact: jsyrigo@yahoo.com.

In addition to founding her own religion (Judyism), comedian **Judy Tenuta** is a star of the film *Butch Camp*, and her comedy albums include *Space Goddessy*. Check her out at www.judytenuta.com.

*

Dr. Terri, a.k.a. Dr. Terri Ryburn-LaMonte, teaches at Illinois State University, has performed at The Funny Bone comedy clubs, and lives in Normal, Illinois, which makes her the only Normal person in this book. Contact: tlrybur@ilstu.edu.

*

Comedian **Tess** has appeared on Comedy Central, *The Jamie Fo Show*, and has been a finalist on NBC's *Last Comic Standing*.

*

Comedian **Lily Tomlin** is an original cast member of *Laugh-In*. She has acted in films that range from *Nashville* to *Orange County*, and appeared on TV series that include *Murphy Brown*. Web site: www.lilytomlin.com

*

Rosie Tran has performed in comedy clubs and colleges across the U.S., including the Hollywood Improv and Gotham Comedy Club in N.Y. Web site: www.rosietran.com.

*

Comedian **Jill Turnbow** has appeared on *Evening at the Improv, Comedy on the Road, Comedy Club Network*, and *Girls' Night Out*.

Rob Twohy is a headlining comedian and the creator of HeyLady.com, a Web site dedicated to the love of comedy. Rob's personal Web site can be found at robtwohy.com.

*

Comedian **Aisha Tyler** has appeared on E!'s *Talk Soup*, as host of the syndicated dating game, *The Fifth Wheel*, and in a guest role on *Friends*. Web site: www.aishatyler.com.

*

Comedian **Sheryl Underwood** has appeared on BET's *Comic View, Comedy Central*, and in the movie *Bulworth*.

*

Comedian **Jennifer Vally** has performed in comedy clubs across the United States and worked as a comedy writer and producer for the *Late, Late Show with Craig Kilborn, The Tonight Show* and the Oxygen Network.

*

Comedian **Luda Vika** has appeared on all the TV shows that celebrate comedy tonality—*Comedy Compadres, Loco Slam*, and *In Living Color*.

*

Christina Walkinshaw is a Canadian comedian and regular at Yuk Yuk's, who is currently performing in Los Angeles. Contact: walklishus@hotmail.com.

Fiona Walsh is an Irish writer, comic, and performer based in New York City. Web site: www.fionawalsh.com.

*

Comedian **Marsha Warfield** played bailiff Roz Russell on the sitcom *Night Court* and later joined the cast of *Empty Nest*.

*

Jayne Warren writes and performs stand-up and sketch comedy, has acted in theater, film, TV, commercials, and is also a vocalist who composes music. Contact: jaynewarren@hotmail.com, Web site: www.jaynewarren.com.

*

Comedian **Damon Wayans** was the star and one of the creators of *In Living Color*, has starred in several movies including *The Last Boy Scout*, and three of his own HBO specials.

*

Lotus Weinstock was a beloved Los Angeles comedian whose comedy career spanned three decades, from her engagement to Lenny Bruce to appearances on *The Tonight Show, Evening at the Improv, Lifetime's Girls Night Out*, and her extensive charity work.

*

Sheila Wenz has appeared on the cable channels Lifetime, A&E, and Comedy Central.

Comedian **Suzanne Westenhoefer** is the star of her own HBO special and CD entitled *Nothing in My Closet but My Clothes*. Web site: www.suzannew.com.

*

Comedian **Basil White** is a weird, scary man-child. Know all at: www.basilwhite.com.

*

Comedian **Grace White** is a middle-aged hippie with a mother who loves her, a father for whom over-eating is an art form, and a stand-up comedy act like no other. Web site: www.gracewhiteproductions.com.

*

Comedian **Dan Whitney**'s Larry the Cable Guy is featured on nearly 200 radio stations nationwide, and has also been seen on Comedy Central's *Blue Collar Comedy*.

*

Comedian **Penny Wiggins** has appeared on *Evening at the Improv* and with the Amazing Jonathon's Las Vegas show.

*

Comedian **Wendy Wilkins** is also an award-winning filmmaker, published writer, and actress whose work includes the movie *Ready To Rumble*, the CBS sitcom *Still Standing*, and the critically-acclaimed, Los Angeles live variety show *Lime*. Contact: ins01@comcast.net.

Comedian **Flip Wilson** was the star of the 1960's television show, *The Flip Wilson Show*, still running on cable.

*

Comedian **Lizz Winstead** is also the creator of Comedy Central's *The Daily Show* and — God help us all—*The Man Show*. But we forgive her, since she's also helped to create the liberal radio network Air America. Web site: www.airamericaradio.com.

*

Comedian **Anita Wise** has also appeared on *Seinfeld*, *The Tonight Show*, and at the Montreal Comedy Festival.

*

Comedian **Steven Wright** has appeared on numerous HBO specials, was a recurring cast member of the sitcom *Mad about You*, and received an Oscar nomination for Best Short Film. Web site: www.stevenwright.com.

*

Comedian **Pamela Yager** has appeared on *Saturday Night Live* and Comedy Central's *Stand Up, Stand Up*. Web site: http://home.earthlink.net/~pyager/.

*

Henny Youngman was a comedian and king of the one-liners whose career ranged from vaudeville and the Catskills to Johnny Carson's *Tonight Show*.

*

Zorba Jevon performs in colleges and clubs, including the Improv and the Comedy Store, and was the winner of the Aspen Comedy Competition. Contact: zorbajvon@hotmail.com.

Judy Brown was a contributing writer and comedy critic for the *L.A. Weekly* for over a dozen years. She has covered the comedy waterfront for *The Los Angeles Times, The New York Times* syndicate, and various other publications. She lives in Santa Monica, California.